WATER
from the
ROCK

WATER

from the

ROCK

Finding God's

Comfort in

the Midst of

Infertility

DONNA GIBBS
BECKY GARRETT
PHYLLIS RABON

MOODY PRESS
CHICAGO

All Scripture quotations, unless otherwise indicated, are taken from the Holy Bible, *New International Version®*. NIV®. Copyright © 1973, 1978, 1984 by International Bible Society. Used by permission of Zondervan Publishing House. All rights reserved.

Scripture quotations marked NKJV are taken from the *New King James Version*. Copyright © 1982 by Thomas Nelson, Inc. Used by permission. All rights reserved.

Scripture quotations marked NASB are taken from the *New American Standard Bible®*, Copyright © 1960, 1962, 1963, 1968, 1971, 1972, 1973, 1975, 1977, 1995 by The Lockman Foundation. Used by permission.

Scripture quotations marked NRSV are from the *New Revised Standard Version* of the Bible, copyright 1946, 1952, and 1971 by the Division of Christian Education of the National Council of the Churches of Christ in the USA. Used by permission. All rights reserved.

Scripture quotations marked RSV are from the *Revised Standard Version* of the Bible, copyright 1946, 1952, and 1971 by the Division of Christian Education of the National Council of the Churches of Christ in the USA. Used by permission. All rights reserved.

Scripture quotations marked KJV are from the King James Version.

Library of Congress Cataloging-in-Publication Data

Gibbs, Donna, 1972–
    Water from the rock : finding God's comfort in the midst of infertility /Donna Gibbs,
Becky Garrett, Phyllis Rabon.
        p. cm.
    ISBN 0-8024-2931-9
    1. Infertility--Religious aspects--Christianity. 2. Consolation. I. Garrett, Becky. II. Rabon,
Phyllis. III. Title.

RC889 .G53 2002
248.8´6196692--dc21

2002070980

1 3 5 7 9 10 8 6 4 2

Printed in the United States of America

To our Lord and Savior Jesus Christ, who strengthens us;
our spouses, who have traveled the hard road with us;
our miracle children,
Braden, Joshua, and Jordan,
who came into the lives of two of the authors during the editing of this book;
and to all couples who have struggled with infertility—
may you be blessed and encouraged in your reading of this book.

CONTENTS

ACKNOWLEDGMENTS

*We gratefully acknowledge Dr. Gary Chapman,
for his insight and suggestions;
our pastor, Dr. Greg T. Mathis,
for his spiritual guidance and loving support;
Elsa Mazon, for her prayers, suggestions, and ideas
and her willingness to work with three novices; and
"To Know" music ministry, for being with us
during our initial speaking engagement as
"Vessels of Freedom" and for being our good friends.*

INTRODUCTION

T he wedding was beautiful. Lifelong hopes and dreams became a reality as the vows were spoken and the couple was introduced to those in attendance. The bride and groom started down the aisle together, full of aspirations for a hope-filled, joyous life together. They pictured themselves living the American dream, with a beautiful home, a Volvo in the garage, and 2.4 children.

Time passed. One year turned into two. Then, suddenly, three, four, and five years passed. Family and friends began to question, "When are you two going to have a baby?" "You know, you're not getting any younger." "Isn't it about time you started having a family?"

As time went on, the couple noticed peers having no difficulty getting pregnant. In fact, the decision to get pregnant seemed as easy for others as the decision to go get groceries. "Get groceries on Thursday; get pregnant on Friday." Yet, for this couple, infertility was becoming a harsh reality. They considered the time, energy, finances, and emotional strain involved in medical interventions or adoption. It was all so confusing and overwhelming. They prayed, questioning God, asking, "Why?" Why was it that their friends were able to so easily get pregnant again, and again, and again? Why was it that walking down the baby food aisle of the grocery store had become so unbearable? Why were announcements of pregnancies and baby showers a slap in the face? Why was Mother's Day such a sad occasion? Why?

Well, my friend, if any of these thoughts stir emotions within you, then you have found a place to settle for a while with new friends who have experienced these struggles. *Water from the Rock* was written as a result of our three individual experiences with infertility. We unite and speak in one voice, sharing our spiritual and relational growth experiences from our storms. *Water from the Rock* is written from both our personal and our professional perspectives. More important, it is written from a Christian perspective and takes an honest look at the crisis of unplanned childlessness.

The American Society for Reproductive Medicine reports that "infertility affects about 6.1 million people in the United States—about 10 percent of the reproductive age population." This statistic is probably a low estimate of the many isolated, hurting couples with few places to turn with their grief. If you have personally experienced the storm of infertility, then you have probably been bombarded with intense emotions. Infertility attacks an individual's sense of self-worth and can place a significant strain on relationships.

Water from the Rock is designed to educate you about the grief process of infertility while also providing specific strategies for coping. At the end of each chapter you will find a series of Application Questions, Victory Verses, and From Hope to Action assignments. We challenge you to begin a notebook specifically for your study. Answer the questions at the end of the chapter, which will give you the chance to apply what you are learning to your own situation. Memorize the Victory Verses and complete the From Hope to Action assignments, which are designed to assist you in practicing healthy coping mechanisms. Remember, the more you invest in the healing of your grief, the more you will gain.

Together, the three of us have come to realize that "in all things God works for the good of those who love him, who have been called according to his purpose" (Romans 8:28). Some of those "things" that work together for good are beautiful, pleasant experiences. Other "things" are painful, raging storms. No doubt, infertility is a painful, raging storm. It is a dream crushed and a loss that must be grieved. *Water from the Rock* addresses those losses while pointing you to a hope not found in the world. This hope, found only in Jesus Christ, heals hurting hearts. You see, Jesus is still in the business of calming storms. Being anchored to Him has worked for us, and we know it will also work for you. Join us as we cling to Him and experience *Water from the Rock*.

PROCESSING INFERTILITY GRIEF

1

DENIAL/SHOCK

"I can't believe this is happening to *me.*"

Charlene and her husband, Ralph, discontinued birth control three years into their marriage. They made preparations for a child in their home and eagerly anticipated a new addition to the family. To prevent interference, they didn't tell friends or relatives about their dreams. Months turned into years, and, as normally happens, others became inquisitive. They began to ask, "When are you two going to have a baby?" Or, "You know, you're not getting any younger—you had better get busy." Still others dropped more subtle hints as they offered their hand-me-down cribs and baby clothes. As the pressure increased, Ralph and Charlene coped by denying their desire for a child. To avoid the pressure, they replied, "Oh, we really don't want to have children."

Denial

After years of trying to become pregnant with no success, many couples may be denying the reality that they have a problem with infertility. That's because approximately 90 percent of couples *are* able to become pregnant after one year of attempts. So what the couple is experiencing is not the norm. Yet the infertile couple in denial may not realize or admit that there is a problem until years later.

Let us make clear that denial is a healthy and necessary coping mechanism for some individuals and couples. It is a normal, and sometimes necessary aspect of the grieving process. It is the inborn safety latch that helps people survive tragedy or disappointment. But denial can become an unhealthy attempt to control the situation. In this chapter we will examine the difference between healthy and unhealthy denial, motivations for denial, and how to move beyond denial into the healing process of infertility grief.

Consider the wife who has just been given the news that her husband was killed in an accident. In the days following his death, she may live as though he is still there. She may continue to fix a plate for him at dinner or save a seat for him at church. Initially she will live her life in denial, unable to comprehend what has just happened to her. If she *could* comprehend it, she would be emotionally overwhelmed. Denial is her safety mechanism—it allows her to survive this tragedy. This same safety mechanism is also accessible during our infertility grief. It allows us to deal with the disappointing news of childlessness until our emotions are prepared to accept the truth.

But the problem with denial is that it is comfortable. It is the easiest of all the grief stages and so the most popular; people like to stay there. That means that many people who are facing infertility remain in denial because it seems so painless even though the safety mechanism of denial is no longer needed. When denial is unnecessarily maintained over a length of time, it becomes unhealthy—a mechanism of destruction, rather than safety.

FEAR

What motivates this unhealthy denial? *Fear.*

We may deny our situation because we *fear rejection.* Remember Ralph and Charlene? They reported a great fear of disappointing loved ones because they were unable to get pregnant. They feared they would no longer be accepted by their friends and family if these people knew they were unable to have children. They also feared rejection from couples at church or at work who didn't understand their dilemma.

Fear of failure will also lead to denial. Charlene feared failing as a woman if she weren't able to conceive.

Some couples may *fear losing their marriage* if they face their infertility. They may be anxious that their relationship cannot bear the emotional strain.

Naturally, we all *fear being hurt and desire to avoid discomfort,* so we may deny our infertility in an attempt to save ourselves from pain.

Last, we may *fear ourselves.* Can we really accept ourselves as infertile? The shame of being unable to conceive combined with the motivation of fear are catalysts for the inactivity that characterizes this stage of denial.

Unhealthy denial is fearfully saying no to the circumstances of life. It is avoiding the truth about what is happening. Unhealthy denial is walking away from the complicated puzzles of life rather than struggling to figure out how the pieces fit together.

HIDDEN GRIEF

Imagine that you have fallen and broken your leg. What will you do? Will you ignore the bone protruding from your pants leg? Will you smile and act as though nothing has happened? Will you fail to mention the broken bone as your friend approaches? Will you feel that you have to wait before receiving medical attention? Will you put off healing by ignoring the problem? Of course not! You will shout about that pain to everyone who will listen, and you will seek medical attention immediately. You won't ignore that broken leg. That's because breaking a bone permits the expression of pain. Similarly, when you experience the death of a loved one, you will go ahead and mourn, because people are expected to mourn such a loss.

However, infertility is a loss that leads to what many professionals refer to as *hidden grief*. It doesn't get expressed publicly. That's because the loss brought about by infertility is not as widely understood as the loss experienced when a loved one dies. Infertility is intangible, whereas death is tangible. Infertility cannot be touched or seen, so its bearers hide their sorrow, complicating their grief and prolonging their healing.

Ralph and Charlene's denial of their infertility became very destructive. In their pride, they hid and denied their desire for children for so long that they almost started believing it themselves. They became confused about what they wanted and who God called them to be. They weren't really sure who they were as a couple. Years later, they learned that life hadn't waited for them to let go of their denial and confusion. Instead, life passed them by, and they lost valuable years. Those were years they could have used to pursue options to their childlessness. Those were years they could have used to move on in their grief and experience emotional and spiritual healing for their loss. Denial didn't *change* their situation. Their life and their infertility continued, even when they refused to acknowledge them.

BROKEN RELATIONSHIPS

When denial and disbelief are maintained long enough, they wear on significant relationships. When one spouse is in denial but the other is not, intense conflict arises. One spouse may be ready to move on, to pray about options, to grieve, and to mourn, but the other doesn't even acknowledge that anything is wrong. The longer this conflict goes on, the more division the couple will have. Pretty soon, they will have two issues to grieve—the loss of a dream and the loss of a relationship.

There may also be division among close friends. It is more difficult to maintain denial when your closest friends are having babies. You may find yourself avoiding them as a way of avoiding the pain of childlessness that you are afraid of feeling. You may find yourself withdrawing, isolating yourself from friends who were once a source of strength and encouragement while inviting in other childless couples who don't interfere with your denial.

The most significant impact of long-term denial is a divided relationship with God. If you are currently in an unhealthy form of denial, you are probably feeling distance between yourself and God. This distance is not because God has moved. It's because God is truth, and you aren't able to acknowledge the truth. God is allowing a situation that you are not accepting. It is not that you are consciously angry with God. When you are in denial, you have nothing to be "angry" about, because "nothing is wrong." Long-term, unhealthy denial requires laying aside faith and rejecting God's work. It is failing to see, through faith, that God can transform a harsh reality into something beautifully acceptable.

Remember Satan's task in this world. He is a deceiver, there is no truth in him, and he seeks to create division (John 8:44; 1 John 2:4). Do you see how Satan could use this stage of grief to cause destruction? Satan will strike to maintain your denial, delay your acceptance of the truth, and keep you from living realistically. He would love to see you in this stage of grief permanently, for when you are in denial he has a better chance of keeping you away from truth and thus apart from God and God's plan for you. As long as Satan keeps you in the grip of denial, he prevents the beautiful promise of transformation Jesus came to give you. This transformation is a release from bondage into the freedom of truth (John 8:32). Keep in mind, as you are reminded in Isaiah 61:3, that Jesus came to heal you as He exchanges your "mourning for joy," your "ashes for beauty," and your "spirit of heaviness" for a "garment of praise."

SHOCK: THE DOOR OUT

So where is the release from this bondage of unhealthy denial? Where is the door out? Well, it is the door out of comfort and into temporary discomfort. It is the door of *shock*. Shock is facing the change that is being forced upon you. Facing this change will challenge your faith and alter your life while opening doors for progress and growth. Shock is like alcohol to an open wound—it hurts as it provides healing. Shock moves you out of denial because it is the recognition of the truth.

In the sudden death of a loved one, shock is actually the first stage of grief; shock is the initial reaction. However, infertility grief has a gradual onset in most cases, which means you will probably experience denial before you experience shock. Still, some couples or individuals may experience shock, or the acceptance of reality, before facing denial.

What types of situations will spark shock in someone who is in the denial stage of infertility grief? Shock could hit with the receipt of new test results. Shock could hit at a class reunion when you learn that you are the only one of your old group of friends who does not have a child. Shock could hit as you walk down the baby food aisle at the grocery store. Shock could hit at a birthday party, at a baby dedication ceremony, on Mother's Day, on Father's Day, at a family get-together, at a baby shower, or as you visit a friend in the maternity ward at the local hospital.

Shock doesn't always hit suddenly, with a devastating blow, but it certainly can. Do you remember Ralph and Charlene? Ralph and Charlene finally came out of their fog of denial, but it wasn't easy. They decided to go to an infertility clinic to have tests run. They were hopeful and excited about this gigantic leap. After years of telling others they didn't want a child, this was a huge step. The doctor did the basic tests on both of them. Ralph had a sperm analysis, and Charlene had a vaginal ultrasound and some blood work. In one devastating hour, they found that Ralph was sterile and Charlene had to have an emergency hysterectomy. All hopes of having a biological child were crushed. *Shock hit.*

Additional losses of life can also shock someone out of a denial of infertility. Some of these losses might be the death of a loved one, a physical illness, or perhaps a miscarriage or a tubal pregnancy. All of these are ingredients for a movement out of denial. Shock may eventually hit with the onset of menopause. Whether gradual or sudden, sooner or later shock is that *something* that spurs a couple out of denial. It is the acknowledgment of the facts, of the difficult reality. Shock is the onset of grief.

Needless to say, shock is uncomfortable. Shock is a state of imbalance, a loss of control, a sense of paralysis. Shock produces emotions that denial may have suppressed, and those emotions usually present themselves all at the same time, in a jumbled mess. It is this flowing of emotions that exposes the darkness of denial and invites the light of true healing to begin.

Have you ever seen someone in a state of physical shock? If so, he has probably just experienced trauma to his body. In his shock, he may be confused or even be convulsing. His body is responding physically to the recent blow. The shock we are describing in this chapter is certainly not this violent, but it is a state of alarm caused by disturbing news. Shock is like a slow-motion dream. All of your senses and emotions are intensely alert, yet it is difficult to distinguish dream from reality. Shock is being so overwhelmed by emotion that you may only be able to murmur or mumble. However, in the case of infertility grief, shock is a good thing; it is the exit out of denial and the entry into healing. It is an essential aspect of the grief process. Shock has a purpose—it introduces the healing process. So with this long-range goal in mind, the discomfort of shock is to be welcomed. *Yes, welcomed.*

CHOOSE TO MOVE

The first stage of the grief process of infertility includes denial and shock. This stage is extremely important because it sets the foundation for how and at what pace you will move through the remainder of the process. If you are in denial about your infertility, you may be afraid to move on with your life. You may be afraid that your tears will never end if you allow yourself to face the facts.

Allow denial to serve its purpose as a safety valve while it needs to, but don't allow yourself to stay there indefinitely. You have a journey ahead of you that is the only road to healing. Yes, you *will* have tears on this journey, but they *will* stop. The destination of healing is worth the journey ahead.

We encourage you, from this point forward, to *choose to move*. You don't have to remain stuck. Fix your eyes on your Savior. Fix your eyes on the One who knows suffering and discomfort. Fix your eyes on *truth*. Fix your eyes on the One who *is* truth. Focus on the *only* One who can heal. With His help, you can—and will—progress through your grief. "I can do everything through him who gives me strength" (Philippians 4:13). Your closeness to Him will be directly related to your progression. He is already at the next stage. He is gently and lovingly reaching back, like a magnet, desiring to pull you toward His healing place. Allow yourself to give up your control so that you can receive the "pull" with the fewest number of stumbles. God desires to bring you through your grief into growth. That *is* truth! Won't you trust Him?

Application Questions

1. *Are you currently in the stage of denial or shock?*
   If so, what symptoms are you experiencing that lead you to this conclusion?

2. *If you have already passed through the stage of denial, think back.*
   Did you stay there for very long? Why or why not?
   Describe your experience with shock. What spurred your exit from denial?
   If you could live this stage over again, what would you do differently?

3. *If you are currently in the stage of denial, how long are you planning on staying there?*
   What will your life be like five years from now if you choose to linger in this stage?
   Why would God not have you in this stage for a long time?
   What specific steps can you take to exit the door of denial into the process of healing?

REMEMBER, DENIAL PROMOTES PROCRASTINATION.
TRUTH PROMOTES PROGRESS.

Victory Verses

"You will know the truth, and the truth will set you free."
—JOHN 8:32

His truth shall be thy shield and buckler.
—PSALM 91:4 KJV

God will never leave thee, nor forsake thee.
—HEBREWS 13:5 KJV

Dear children, let us not love with words or tongue
but with actions and in truth.
—1 JOHN 3:18

FROM HOPE TO ACTION

Denial is a tool for coping with grief. Your action assignment is to pray about and list other healthy tools you can use to help you cope when you begin living in the reality of your loss. Some examples might be prayer, Bible study, fellowship with other Christians, physical exercise, and eating nutritiously.

2

DESPERATION/PANIC

"I'll do whatever it takes to have a child."

Now Sarai, Abram's wife, had borne him no children. But she had an Egyptian maidservant named Hagar, so she said to Abram, "The Lord has kept me from having children. Go, sleep with my maidservant; perhaps I can build a family through her."

Abram agreed to what Sarai said. So after Abram had been living in Canaan ten years, Sarai his wife took her Egyptian maidservant Hagar and gave her to her husband to be his wife. He slept with Hagar, and she conceived. (Genesis 16:1–4)

Wow, talk about desperation. Sarai (later called Sarah) so grieved her loss that she rejected all sense of rationality. She was so afraid of being childless forever that she felt the need to take control. She took the driver's seat in her life, although she hadn't thought about where the road might lead. She made a drastic decision of disobedience even after she had already been given a promise by God that her childlessness would not be permanent.

At this particular time in her life, Sarai was in the *second stage* of the process of infertility grief, *desperation and panic*. As you can probably guess, this stage is a dangerous one. In Sarai's desperation, she was able to focus only on her immediate desires. She wanted a child *now;* she was tired of waiting on God's promise. She felt as though God had forgotten about her and that if she were ever to have a child, she would have to take the matter into her own hands.

With little thought involved, Sarai ran to her first option, her maid-servant. She never thought about how this decision would affect her relationship with Abram (later called Abraham). She never considered the impact of this action on her relationship with Hagar. She never weighed the possible influence this decision would have on the child that Hagar bore. She had the shortsighted view typical of desperation. She panicked because she felt her time and her options had run their course.

Perhaps you have never sent your spouse to have intercourse with another person in hopes of "achieving" a family, but I'm sure you have felt at least a slight sensation of panic if you have or are facing infertility. You may be able to relate to the fear that drove Sarai's impulsive decision. Your fear may display itself in an obsession with temperature charts or ovulation predictor kits. Or it may display itself in routine, forced sexual encounters with your spouse, all in hopes of obtaining a child.

Regardless of the level of impact of this stage on your life, we challenge you to pay close attention to this chapter. Our fleshly natures leave us all susceptible to this stage, even in the best of situations. Take note of the characteristics that describe this stage and take a close look at your own struggles in order to gauge how much power your desperation over infertility has on your life.

CHARACTERISTICS OF DESPERATION/PANIC

1. *The central focus of your life becomes achieving pregnancy.* Most of your thoughts are devoted to this issue. You are constantly contemplating possible ways to succeed in conceiving. This focus may even involve extensive and disruptive daydreaming or fantasizing about becoming pregnant. Your focus is on the short-term and the immediate.

Example: During the days approaching and following ovulation, Tina found it practically impossible to concentrate at work. She could hear people talking to her, but all she could think about was what was happening (or not happening) to her body. She was in a daze, and her mind could only focus on her fertility endeavors. She would forget things she was told. She even lost interest in other areas of her life because she was so focused on her quest for a baby.

★PANIC PROMOTES IRRATIONAL, IMPULSIVE BEHAVIORS.

2. *You take an aggressive approach to medical interventions.* During the desperation stage, patients facing infertility get to know their doctors very well. In fact, "aggressive" is probably the understatement of the year. Money is no object when you are scared. Physical consequences are irrelevant when you are panicked. Nothing matters—just give me whatever will increase my chances of conception.

Example: Drew and Lilly have tried to have a child for two years. Lilly has just turned thirty-four and is worried about the possibility of birth defects if they do not get pregnant soon. Against their doctor's recommendation, they have undergone in vitro fertilization three months in a row. They already have over $35,000 in debt just from the last few months of treatment. In addition, Lilly's health is in jeopardy because of the swelling of her ovaries and because she has developed cysts as a result of the injectable medications she has received.

★PANIC PROMOTES IRRATIONAL, IMPULSIVE BEHAVIORS.

3. *You compromise personal convictions in order to meet the goal of pregnancy.* Fear is not of God (2 Timothy 1:7). So when we are afraid, we are vulnerable to sin. Unfortunately, during this stage of the grief process, we may set aside convictions and morals to justify an action that produces the result we feel we need. In an effort to carry out this compromise, we may surround ourselves with people who won't call attention to the moral issues but will freely assist us in our endeavor. At the same time, we will block out those who will hold us accountable to our convictions.

Example: When Gina and Tom first learned of Tom's infertility, they discussed various medical interventions with their doctor. Gina told the physician about her convictions regarding using a sperm donor. She said that she had done a lot of praying and studying concerning this option and did not believe it was God's desire for them. She urged the doctor to explore other options. A year later, new test results reported that Gina's husband was actually sterile. The possibility of never experiencing pregnancy floored Gina, and, without her husband's knowledge, she made an appointment to speak with the physician about a sperm donor.

PANIC PROMOTES IRRATIONAL, IMPULSIVE BEHAVIORS.

4. *You begin to neglect other responsibilities.* Because the dream of a child is so intense during this stage of grief, it overpowers other duties and redistributes what may have at one time been a balanced life. Priorities get shifted during the stage of desperation. In panic, fertility becomes the top priority. Fertility demands more time, energy, and resources than any other aspect of life during this stage. The result may be that you miss job deadlines or ignore your spouse's needs.

Example: Elizabeth and her husband, Todd, are facing secondary infertility. They have one child, Marie, who is five years old, but they have been unable to have a second child. Recently, Elizabeth has been consumed by thoughts of having another child. She has just begun a trial of clomiphene, with hopes of assisting conception through medical intervention. She has taken off work almost every day this month out of fear of overstressing her body. She is so afraid of straining her body that she has spent most of her time being inactive. This fear has also had a large impact on Elizabeth's relationship with her daughter, who is starting to feel neglected and ignored by her mother.

PANIC PROMOTES IRRATIONAL, IMPULSIVE BEHAVIORS.

5. *You make impulsive decisions.* Have you ever seen someone in a state of panic make a well-thought-out decision? Probably not, and you probably won't see many wise decisions made in this stage of impulsiveness. There is a state of urgency during this stage, a sense of hurriedness. Consider a child who has Attention Deficit Hyperactivity Disorder (ADHD). That child's behavior is characterized by impulsiveness. Whatever he wants, whatever he has on his mind, he goes for it without much thought of the consequences. Children with ADHD often get hurt because of their impulsiveness. In their rush, they don't take the time to think about the possible harm they may endure.

In the stage of desperation and panic, you could say that couples with infertility also have ADHD. They are inclined to run after what they want, regardless of what they have been told. They may make spontaneous, hasty, and sometimes irresponsible decisions regarding their childlessness. Unfortunately, those decisions may be harmful or hurtful. At the very least, they will probably yield discomfort.

> *Example:* Jennifer and Lee celebrated their fifteenth wedding anniversary last year. Their anniversary was a reminder to them that the years were moving along quickly and they were still childless. They decided on a whim to go to a meeting at a local adoption agency. At that meeting they learned of several children waiting for adoption. Things happened very quickly, and before they fully realized what was happening, they were in the process of adopting a child.
>
> They did not pray about the decision, nor did they think through the pros and cons of the course they were about to take. In an effort to assure that they would have the best opportunity to adopt, they agreed to an open adoption. They are now regretting that they did not take more time to contemplate their decision. The birth mother is not a Christian and disagrees with them over how they should raise their child. This relationship has been conflictual and stressful. They love their child dearly and do not regret bringing him into their home, but each day they face the consequences of a decision made in haste.

PANIC PROMOTES IRRATIONAL, IMPULSIVE BEHAVIORS.

6. *If you are a Christian, you may begin to neglect your relationship with God.* God desires to be first in our lives, but when any area of life becomes an obsession, God is *not* first. Our first priority is the focus of our panic. We put God on the back burner and let our desire for a child take precedence over a relationship with Him. During the stage of desperation, pregnancy may become an idol (Colossians 3:5). We attempt to take control away from God and give it to ourselves.

> *Example:* Teresa became a Christian when she was seventeen. Since then, she has walked closely with the Lord, with a yearning and hunger for a deeper relationship with Him. However, her husband, Randy, has noticed recently she has stopped spending time in prayer and Bible study. She has also quit going to church. When he asks her about this change, she becomes defensive and says she doesn't want to talk about it. Finally, Teresa admits to Randy that she knows she is neglecting her relationship with God. She tells him that when she spends time with God, she is convicted over her obsession with achieving a pregnancy, and yet she cannot face giving up control over this part of her life.

PANIC PROMOTES IRRATIONAL, IMPULSIVE BEHAVIORS.

7. *You experience extreme emotional responses.* During the stage of desperation and panic, life is lived in absolutes. "I *have* to get pregnant this month." "I *must* have a child, or my life will not be complete." When your entire world is dependent on one seemingly unreachable goal, you will become frazzled and confused. In your efforts to be in control, you will lose control. When things don't work out the way you have planned, you will become anxious, irritable, angry, and depressed. Panic is not a comfortable place to be.

> *Example:* Julie and Tim have worked out every detail of their efforts to achieve pregnancy this month. Tim feels that the endeavor

is under control and proceeding smoothly. However, Julie has con-
fided to her pastor that she feels as if she is going insane. She is
feeling emotions she never knew existed—and feeling them all at
once. She cries sometimes, yells at other times, and always feels
nervous and anxious. She describes her life as a hurried time
bomb and her efforts to gain control as trying to swim through
molasses. The couple's hurried decisions and attempts to achieve
pregnancy are more than she can handle.

PANIC PROMOTES IRRATIONAL, IMPULSIVE BEHAVIORS.

NEW PROBLEMS IN PLACE OF THE OLD

Consider each of these characteristics in light of Sarai's testimony.
In her desperation, she exhibited them all. Her central focus was to have
a child and increase her family. Her identity was wrapped up in that
goal. It was all she could think about. The Bible does not state the point
specifically, but she probably fantasized about what it would be like to
be a mother. She may have spent countless hours mentally comparing
herself to other women who were mothers. Sarai was also aggressive in
her approach to her situation. She might not have had a reproductive en-
docrinologist available, but she was forceful in her intervention. Sarai
compromised her convictions. She set aside what was right to meet her
immediate want.

Sarai also probably neglected other areas of her life. It is likely that
because she was so focused on this void she was unable to give the blessings in her life the attention they deserved. In her pursuit of "completeness" to erase her barrenness, she put aside her relationship with God
and His promise to her and made an impulsive, detrimental decision. She
tried to gain control of her emotions with a quick fix. If you read further in Genesis 16, you will learn that Sarai faced difficult consequences
for her panicky decision. In her attempt to solve her problem by herself, she created new ones.

Have you created "new problems" in your urgency to have a child?
In your state of desperation, your obsession with pregnancy is all-

consuming and the ramifications of the obsession irrelevant. Your focus is simple: "Hurry, Hurry, Hurry!" "Me, Me, Me!" "Baby, Baby, Baby!" You will do whatever it takes in your quest for a baby.

Trouble in Your Marriage

If you are currently in the midst of this stage of the grief process, you are probably blind to those new problems you may be creating. How is your marriage? Are you communicating? Does your mate feel loved? Are you investing in the love relationship with your precious spouse to the same extent as your investment in conception? At this stage in the storm of infertility, the beautiful sexual relationship between a husband and wife is threatened as it is sometimes replaced with a timed ritual that becomes part of the quest for a baby. How is your lovemaking? Is it a beautiful physical and emotional experience, or is it a technical, stressful act to be dreaded?

Be aware that Satan's task on this earth is division. Because you may be distracted by your mission, you may be more vulnerable to his attacks on your marriage in this stage. Satan desires to divide you from your spouse and break up your home. Be aware and on guard. Remember, you have victory in the One who is more powerful than Satan, and you don't have to succumb to Satan's attempts to destroy. If you have already wrought some damage to your marriage relationship, keep reading. Later in this book, you will be given specific strategies for restoring wounded relationships.

Financial Problems

Another new problem often created in this stage is financial debt. In desperation, many of us take desperate measures. Many couples have run up credit card debt, borrowed against their home, or taken all of their savings and spent them in this quest. When you are in a state of panic, you may make major financial decisions without prayer or deliberation. Unfortunately, you may already have frivolously spent thousands of dollars in your desperate plea for a child. You now live in regret, with an additional strain of debt placed on your marriage. If this describes you, keep reading and don't give up in your situation. God can deliver you and prevent you from continuing to make a bad situation worse.

Problems in Your Relationship with God

The most detrimental new problem we can create in this stage of desperation and panic is withdrawing from God. It is at this stage of grief that our relationship with our heavenly Father is threatened as we attempt to put our lives on our timetable instead of His. Our taking control is often spurred by our sense of inadequacy and our fear that we will never be complete without a child. We fear that God's permanent plan for us is childlessness—and that is an unbearable thought at this point in the process.

If you are at this stage of grief, you may have put God on the back burner. Maybe your need for control is so intense that there is no room in your heart for God. You may feel so panicked or so afraid of running out of time that you have given up on God's timetable and are doing whatever you can do to take charge and create results for yourself. Let us warn you, the more you try to gain control, the more you try to take your life into your own hands, the more out of control you will become. In your effort to create results, you will create even more desperation and panic.

YOU DON'T HAVE TO STAY IN DESPERATION

Thankfully, we have some wonderful news for you. This stage of desperation is *completely optional!* You do not have to go through it. If you are in it now, you don't have to stay there. *Choose to move!* If you are a Christian, you are able with Christ's help to overcome your desperation. Exercise the fruit of the Holy Spirit with which all Christians are equipped. According to Galatians 5:22–23, God has specifically provided you with patience and self-control, the exact opposites of desperation and panic.

If you have done some damage in your frantic panic, take a deep breath and get busy on repairs. Don't allow your desperate plea for a child to distract you from God's purposes for you and from the blessings with which He has surrounded you. Ask God to remove the blinders. Prayerfully answer the questions below regarding your experience in this stage of infertility grief.

Application Questions

1. *Are you currently in the stage of desperation and panic?*
    If so, what symptoms are you experiencing that lead you to this conclusion?
    What will your life be like if you continue to linger in this stage?

2. *If you have previously experienced this stage of grief, what "new problems" did your panic create?*
    How did your desperation affect your marriage?
    Your finances?
    Your sense of self?
    Your relationship with God?

3. *What are the potential long-term consequences of your panic?*

Victory Verses

For God hath not given us the spirit of fear; but of power,
and of love, and of a sound mind.
—2 TIMOTHY 1:7 KJV

For God is not the author of confusion, but of peace.
—1 CORINTHIANS 14:33 KJV

FROM HOPE TO ACTION

Discipline yourself with the fruit of the
Spirit of *self-control.* Pray to surrender to
God's desires regarding your childlessness.
Exercise the fruit of *patience* by choosing to
place yourself in God's waiting room. Your
action assignment is to make no major or
minor decisions without God's input.

3

ANGER/RESENTMENT

"What kind of God would
allow me to go through *this?*"

In the last chapter, we discussed the characteristics of the stage of desperation. A characteristic of that stage is to experience extreme emotional responses. One of those emotional responses is anger, which is the focus of this chapter. *Merriam-Webster's New Collegiate Dictionary* defines anger as "a strong passion or emotion of displeasure, and usually antagonism, excited by a sense of injury or insult." In this chapter we will discuss two different types of anger, motivations for anger, and strategies for overcoming unresolved anger related to infertility. We invite you to examine yourself as you peruse this chapter, asking God to help you discern in your own life the presence of anger and its effects.

WARRANTED ANGER AND
UNWARRANTED ANGER

If you have always thought of anger as negative or sinful, you may have been deceived. There are actually two different types of anger: warranted and unwarranted. *Warranted* anger is anger that is justified. It is anger that comes about in response to a wrongdoing that clearly needs amending.

Jesus gave us an example of warranted anger in Matthew 21:12–13 when He learned of the misuse of the temple for deceptive trading and unmerited profit. His anger was warranted, just, and righteous because God's house was being defiled and because people were being treated unfairly. Jesus demonstrated a sinless expression of righteous anger as He confronted the money changers and overthrew their tables. His anger energized Him to act in order to bring about justice for those receiving unacceptable treatment.

In contrast, *unwarranted* anger is anger that is not justified. If acted on, unwarranted anger results in sin. A biblical example of unwarranted anger appears in Genesis 29–30. Two sisters, Rachel and Leah, competed for the love of their husband, Jacob, and for the pride of bearing his offspring. Even though Rachel had Jacob's love, Leah bore his children. Rachel's competitive desperation for a child led to jealousy and anger. Her anger resulted in improper, sinful actions. She worsened her situation by presenting her handmaid to Jacob as a way of deceptively gaining her own offspring. Rachel's jealousy and anger were unwarranted because she resented her barrenness, something over which only God had control (Genesis 30:2).

BENEFICIAL AND DETRIMENTAL
RESPONSES TO ANGER

Anger, warranted or unwarranted, can lead to beneficial or detrimental responses. *Beneficial* responses are those that allow anger to be put to good use. They address injustice and right wrongs with Christ-like actions. *Detrimental* responses do none of these things. They are sinful and make bad situations worse.

Many people who believe that life begins at conception experience warranted anger as they see women choosing abortion. This *warranted* anger can result in *beneficial* or *detrimental* actions. Some people who are angered by abortion choose to use their anger constructively to educate, nurture, and counsel women who face unplanned or unwanted pregnancies. This action is beneficial in that it expresses care and concern for both the mother and the unborn child, while saving lives. Other people, who feel the same warranted anger regarding abortion, choose to respond detrimentally. In their anger, they may worsen a horrific situation by threatening the lives of the doctors who perform abortions. This type of detrimental response brings about further injustice, rather than promoting justice.

MOTIVATIONS FOR INFERTILITY ANGER

What does this distinction between diffferent types of anger have to do with infertility? If you have experienced childlessness, perhaps you have been angry with God because He has allowed you to experience your loss. Maybe you have been angry with your physician, who just could not "make it happen." You may have been angry with your spouse because his physical problems have complicated your efforts to get pregnant. You may have been angry with perfect strangers, who seemed to flaunt their pregnancies simply by walking beside you in the mall. Or maybe you are angry with yourself and see yourself as "incomplete" because of your inability to reproduce.

What do these angers have in common? They are all unwarranted. In fact, much of the anger we feel toward our childlessness is unwarranted because it is misdirected. Do you think your physician is *really* trying to keep you from getting pregnant? Do you *really* think your spouse is happy to have a low sperm count just to disappoint you? Do pregnant women *really* seek you out? Are you *really* incomplete because of your infertility? These questions may seem harsh, but, if you are honest, you can probably answer no to all of them. If so, you may be needlessly expending an excessive amount of energy in this stage of grief.

SAM AND ALICE

Sam and Alice have been married for five years. Six months ago, they pursued infertility testing. Alice's test results were all positive, indicating that she could likely conceive and carry a child. However, Sam learned that he was sterile, which will prevent them from becoming pregnant. As a result, Alice's anger over their infertility has caused her to become resentful of Sam. She blames him for their childlessness. Alice's loss of her dream for a child is very real—but her anger toward Sam is unwarranted. She is unfairly faulting Sam for something over which he has no control. Her anger toward Sam because of his sterility has led her to act unkindly toward him. She has said demeaning, hurtful words to him. She has avoided intimacy with him. She has even contemplated an extramarital affair in order to achieve her goal of a pregnancy. Needless to say, Alice's angry reactions to their infertility have damaged their marriage relationship.

Alice's anger could lead her to beneficial responses. She could *join in oneness* with Sam as they face their fertility obstacles. She could *pray for* Sam. She could *pray with* Sam about their options for a childless marriage. She could *verbally uplift and encourage* Sam, realizing that she could just as easily have been the one who received the diagnosis that meant they couldn't conceive a child. In other words, Alice could *choose* to exercise countless beneficial reactions to her anger. Those choices could bring about healing rather than division and resentment. Her anger could be used in a purposeful rather than a destructive way.

PREGNANT FRIENDS

Another example of infertility anger is demonstrated in the journal entry one of us wrote in the midst of our own anger regarding infertility:

Journal Entry: Tuesday

There was something very difficult about today. I managed to be shown two different ultrasounds by two friends in just one day. Both friends are very aware of our situation and the pain we experience with infertility. I was fine with the first one, but when my second friend began showing me hers . . . and her belly . . . and her book for expectant mothers (because it describes how "we" are), and ugh!! I felt so angry and so hurt. I felt I would explode into tears.

I hate my reaction, but I also feel she had a very self-centered approach . . . all she ever discusses with me is her pregnancy, how wonderful it is for her, and her hopes and dreams for her life with this child. It is a very one-sided conversation that is occasionally interrupted by my futile attempts to change the subject when I feel I cannot take it any more. Even then, somehow it always comes back to the same discussion. Never am I asked how I am doing . . . it's constantly about her and her pregnancy.

You know, I sometimes wonder if all of these pregnancies around me are God allowing Satan to test me, just as he did Job. God, if this is the case, I pray I will soon be relieved of the testing. I don't understand why this gift is being deprived from us and why, when You have the power to place people in our lives, You chose these people, who are a constant reminder of what we try so hard for but can't seem to have.

Was my friend purposely making inconsiderate remarks? Or was she simply unaware of how I was receiving her comments? Whatever the case, I (Donna) had warranted anger because I was hurt by my friend's lack of compassion. But I also had unwarranted anger based on my *perception* and *assumption* that my friend was *trying* to be hurtful. There were many possible detrimental and beneficial responses to this situation. I could have gone into a rage as my friend talked about her pregnancy.

I could have called her names or harshly confronted her over her lack of understanding. I could have ignored my friend or even avoided her completely.

Or I could have celebrated with my friend as she shared her exciting news while also tactfully sharing my own feelings of hurt. This open sharing would not only have strengthened our relationship but also educated my friend about the pain of infertility, increasing her level of understanding and empathy. At the same time, this open sharing would have increased my own understanding of my friend's emotions as she experienced this exciting change in her life. In other words, my anger toward my friend could have been used as a catalyst for beneficial action.

KIMBERLY AND JOHN

Kimberly and John struggled to get pregnant for four years prior to her miscarriage. She had carried the baby three months when she began to have complications. She was immediately flooded with intense anger toward God, who she felt had given her this gift only to cruelly take it away. She secluded herself from her Christian friends and from God. She shook her fist at Him and denounced her faith.

Kimberly faced a significant and upsetting loss—but her anger toward God was unwarranted. A more beneficial, healing response would have been to face her mourning while leaning on God, knowing that He was in control. Her disappointment could have pulled her closer to God through prayer and study, rather than pushing her away. Through her suffering, she could have embraced her loss and drawn strength and comfort from God as never before. Instead of being angry toward Him, her anger toward her loss could have been made useful. It could have motivated her to grieve and, later, maybe even to minister to others going through the same trial.

UNRESOLVED ANGER

Some anger lies at a surface level, but what if your anger regarding infertility lies deeper? What if it has buried itself and become prolonged and intense? That is what we call *unresolved anger*. Unresolved anger will keep you "stuck." Have you ever seen someone who just looks like an angry person? You can see it in his face. Anger ages people and shortens their lives. So also, unresolved anger grows into resentment and bitterness that causes people to have a negative worldview. This anger bleeds into all areas of their lives, affecting their daily functioning and relationships. People with unresolved anger expect the worst. They are pessimistic and discouraged. The Bible says, "See to it that no one misses the grace of God and that no bitter root grows up to cause trouble and defile many" (Hebrews 12:15). Anger can become a stumbling block for others (Romans 14:13).

Prolonged, rooted anger will poison your thoughts, emotions, self-worth, decisions, and relationships. Persistent anger will distort your thinking—and this distorted thinking will lead to destructive actions. Proverbs 23:7 (KJV) says, "For as he thinketh in his heart, so is he." Your angry thoughts and behavior *will become who you are*. Unresolved anger will destroy you and your future and adversely affect those around you. Time is of the essence. If you can see yourself in this paragraph, you may have unresolved anger that has taken root. This root will only grow deeper and stronger. Be active in uprooting it. Ask God, through the Holy Spirit, to destroy and remove the roots of your anger. Then keep reading to learn other specific strategies to gain freedom.

Unresolved anger often leads to irrational thoughts and behavior. You have probably heard of the term *road rage*. Maybe you have even seen or felt the effects of this phenomenon on the Interstate.

I (Donna) remember one time when my husband and I were traveling out of town. A man in the lane next to us began blowing his horn, flailing his arms, and screaming at the top of his lungs. He even tried to sideswipe us as we traveled down the highway. Apparently, he thought we had wronged him, or perhaps he held unresolved anger about something else altogether and took it out on us. I never understood what precipitated his angry outburst, but I gather he blamed us for something that had delayed or inconvenienced him.

A similar, irrational anger can display itself with infertility. What if we called this kind of anger *baby rage?* Perhaps your quest for a baby is the central focus of your life. You have not been able to become pregnant —and now you are angry. This anger may persist and become *baby rage*. This baby rage, like road rage, will lead to impatience, blame, and unforgiveness. It can also lead to irrational thoughts and conclusions. It will surely lead to a negative attitude, negative speech, and negative behavior.

Just as uncontrolled road rage can end in disaster, so too, uncontrolled baby rage can lead to disaster. It can even lead to outbursts of anger or stored anger that is damaging to the physical or emotional self. Baby rage is buying the lie that something or someone is to blame for your pain.

This rage may not be obvious. In road rage, a person's anger may be directed toward people who really have not offended him. Similarly, your baby rage might take itself out on people and situations that are totally unrelated to your infertility. Infertility anger, left unresolved, will spread into all areas of your life, leaving you with a negative, pessimistic outlook.

Do you have unresolved anger in your heart? Consider your thought patterns for a moment. Are they harmful and hurtful or hopeful and helpful? Are your actions destructive or constructive? Is anger guiding you, or are you guided by the Holy Spirit? If you have recognized that you are harboring unresolved anger toward yourself, God, or other people, you probably are ready to get rid of it. You can probably list the harms this anger has caused you and others. You probably want some relief from your anger.

STRATEGIES FOR MOVING BEYOND ANGER

How can you move beyond infertility anger? If God created the emotion of anger, how can you transform it so that it is used in a helpful way?

1. *Identify whether your anger is warranted or unwarranted.* Examine the true source of your anger. What is really motivating this feeling? Are you making assumptions that are incorrect? Examine your beliefs and thoughts about your infertility.

2. *If you determine that your anger is unwarranted, be thankful.* There is no reason for you to continue to carry this burden of anger. Confess your anger to God and to anyone else it has affected.

But if you determine that your anger is warranted, which in the case of infertility will be in only a few isolated cases, then you have to choose between two options—confronting the wrong and being willing to forgive or not confronting the wrong and being willing to forgive. Notice that, as Christians, forgiveness is our only option for overcoming unresolved anger. God reminds us in Matthew 6:12 to forgive others just as He has forgiven us. Forgiveness is not a feeling; it is a decision. Whom do you need to decide to forgive, even if you don't feel like it? Conquering unresolved anger is just that: a decision.

3. *Make sure that God, and not your infertility, is the central focus of your life.* Who gets more time and attention from you, God or your anger? Cling to your faith rather than your feelings, trusting that your feelings will follow. Hang on to God and focus your prayers on your freedom from the bondage of long-lasting anger. Ask God to replace your anger with the fruit of the Spirit (Galatians 5:22–23).

4. *Get out of your box and look around at what other people might be facing in their lives.* Choose to reach out to them; choose to better understand their pain. This broadening of your focus will allow you to exercise the fruit of the Spirit as you take the focus off of your own loss and minister to someone else in her pain.

5. *Allow yourself to laugh.* Laughter is great therapy. "A merry heart doeth good like a medicine," the Scriptures remind us (Proverbs 17:22 KJV). Find some humor in walking through the hospital at the same time the Lamaze class lets out. Find some humor in having to travel through the baby food aisle to get to the toothpaste. When you run across a person or a situation that normally brings out your anger, focus your energy on finding some humor. Laughter is healing; anger is defeating.

HANNAH

All of this sounds fine and dandy, but is it really possible to experience the intense grief of infertility without being overwhelmed by feelings of resentment and anger? Is it really possible to have righteous anger and righteous actions in light of deep sorrow? Absolutely!

Turn with us to 1 Samuel 1:1–2:10. We will visit with Hannah, who was married to Elkanah. Elkanah had another wife, Peninnah, and Peninnah had two children. The Bible states that God closed Hannah's womb. But despite Hannah's barrenness, Elkanah loved Hannah genuinely and paid her extra attention, lavishing her with gifts, while Peninnah hurled insults her way. Hannah's life was greatly affected by this abuse, and she grieved for years.

Month after month, year after year, God said no, and Hannah endured the jeers of a society that did not understand or appreciate her situation. Put yourself in Hannah's position. Perhaps she had feelings of anger toward God, who allowed her to be barren in a society that measured women according to their fertility. Surely she felt anger toward the community of people who rejected her. Mostly, she must have felt anger toward Peninnah, who made fun of her and caused her grief.

Some of Hannah's anger was warranted, and some of it was unwarranted. However, she *never* acted in a detrimental way. She turned to God with such intense prayer that the priest who sat nearby thought she was intoxicated. Hannah begged for a child, knowing that only the Creator had the power to answer her request. She begged for relief from her situation.

Can you imagine the sincerity and depth of Hannah's prayers as she poured out her heart to God, praying for deliverance from her anger and sadness? Hannah walked with grace, *choosing* not to stoop to Peninnah's level of abuse. She could have even prayed for God to harm Peninnah as a payback, but we hear none of that in Scripture. Instead, Hannah focused her prayers on herself and asked God to help her deal with Peninnah's unfair treatment (1 Samuel 1:11).

In the end, not only did God heal Hannah's emotional wounds, He healed her physical womb and blessed her with a son she called Samuel.

Though God may not grant your request for a biological child, we challenge you to give Him your burden of anger in the same way Hannah did and watch to see what He will give you in return.

Application Questions

1. *Which form of anger (warranted or unwarranted) do you notice most in your life?*

2. *Think of a time when you felt unwarranted anger about your infertility (perhaps toward yourself, God, or others). What were your actions? Did you use your anger for a beneficial or a detrimental purpose? What was the outcome?*

3. *Have you experienced persistent, unresolved anger? Why or why not? What will you choose to do with it?*

Victory Verses

Be ye angry, and sin not: let not the sun go down upon your wrath: neither give place to the devil.
—EPHESIANS 4:26–27 KJV

Let all bitterness, and wrath, and anger, and clamour, and evil
speaking, be put away from you, with all malice: and be ye
kind one to another, tenderhearted, forgiving one another,
even as God for Christ's sake hath forgiven you.
—EPHESIANS 4:31–32 KJV

Beloved, avenge not yourselves, but rather give place unto
wrath: for it is written, Vengeance is mine;
I will repay, saith the Lord.
—ROMANS 12:19 KJV

FROM HOPE TO ACTION

Make a list of all the people toward whom
you feel anger related to your infertility.
Write a letter to each one—not necessarily
to be given to them but to be used to help
you face and vent your anger. If anger has
scarred your emotions, make a decision to
become healed by forgiving your offender.
Write out your decision in this letter.

4

⌒

SADNESS/DEPRESSION

"Why me?"

"Jesus wept" (John 11:35). Of course He wept. As he stood at the tomb of His beloved friend Lazarus, He "was deeply moved in spirit and troubled" (v. 33). Seeing His friends mourn, and feeling His own loss, He went to the depths of grief. He cried over His loss. We know that His grief over Lazarus moved those surrounding Him because the Scriptures tell us that they said, "See how he loved him!" (v. 36).

Another example of Jesus' deep sorrow occurred in the Garden of Gethsemane on the Mount of Olives as He faced taking upon Himself the sins of the world. "And being in anguish, he prayed more earnestly, and his sweat was like drops of blood falling to the ground" (Luke 22:44). This verse refers to the time Jesus prayed in the hours just before His arrest. His anguish was so intense that He experienced hematidrosis, which the *Dictionary of Science and Technology* (Harcourt) describes as "an extremely rare disorder characterized by excretion of blood or blood pigment in the sweat."

Matthew recorded Jesus as saying, "My soul is overwhelmed with sorrow to the point of death" (26:38). Jesus was not exaggerating about His grief. Our research shows only ten reported cases of hematidrosis in history, all the result of severe anguish. All ten of the sufferers died. In Isaiah 53:3, Jesus is described as a "man of sorrows, and familiar with suffering." Can you relate to Jesus? He can certainly relate to you!

SORROW IN OTHER PARTS OF THE BIBLE

Not only Jesus, but many other biblical characters experienced sorrow and depression.

Hannah

We have already talked about Hannah and her struggle with barrenness (1 Samuel 1:1–2:10). We would encourage you to study her story. She experienced sorrow over barrenness for years, when month after month God said no to her pleas for a child. Her sadness continued until she was no longer able to accomplish daily life-tasks. She reached such a deep level of depression over her infertility that she stopped eating. At one point, Hannah's pain was so acute that she could not even voice her prayers. "Hannah was praying in her heart, and her lips were moving but her voice was not heard" (1:13).

Have you ever been so sad that you could not find words to pray? Take comfort, knowing that the Holy Spirit intercedes for you when you don't know how to pray (Romans 8:26), just as He interceded for Hannah.

Job

You may be familiar with Job, who is remembered for his struggle with sorrow over the losses that befell him. So deeply grieved was he that he said, "Why did I not perish at birth. . . . Or why was I not hidden in the ground like a stillborn child. . . . I loathe my very life" (Job 3:11, 16; 10:1). Job experienced deep sadness and depression in his weariness with life.

Maybe you have been so distraught about your circumstances that you questioned God's purpose in creating you. Job couldn't see beyond his situation, but God obviously had a purpose for his suffering and a plan for his life. This purpose not only matured Job but also every believer who has studied his sufferings. God's plan for you is no less significant than His plan for Job. "For I know the thoughts that I think toward you, saith the Lord, thoughts of peace, and not of evil, to give you an expected end" (Jeremiah 29:11 KJV). There is hope in our sadness.

Elijah

In 1 Kings 19, the prophet Elijah feared that his life was in danger—and his fear brought him great sorrow. He was tremendously discouraged and felt that life was not worth living. "I have had enough, LORD. . . . Take my life" (v. 4). Forty days later, in his distress, he escaped to a cave and set up residence in the darkness (vv. 8–9). Two times the Lord asked him, "What are you doing here?" (vv. 9, 13). Elijah was so consumed by his sorrows that he lost sight of where God wanted him to be. Have you also found yourself overburdened with your life-trial? Maybe you felt that isolation was the solution. If so, may we ask you the question God asked of Elijah? "What are you doing here?" Have you established residence in your sadness?

Judas Iscariot

Even Judas Iscariot, hard as he was, must have experienced overwhelming sorrow when He realized the extent of his sin. Unfortunately, he found his sin to be more than he could bear. He became irrational in his sorrow and so consumed with it that he took his own life. The Scriptures say that Judas was "seized with remorse" when he saw the result of his actions (Matthew 27:3). He didn't realize that he could go back to God and be forgiven.

Maybe, like Judas, you too have felt hopeless. Maybe you have entertained thoughts of suicide. Yet even Judas, who betrayed our Savior, could have experienced freedom in forgiveness. As 1 John 1:9 states, "If we confess our sins, he is faithful and just and will forgive us our sins and purify us from *all* unrighteousness" (italics added). You can have a clean slate with Christ. Don't allow fluctuating feelings of sadness to distort the stability of your faith.

SORROW IS NORMAL

If Jesus experienced great sorrow, and if the Bible is filled with others who did, it must be normal. God tells us in Ecclesiastes 3:4 that there is "a time to weep and a time to laugh, a time to mourn and a time to dance." In other words, sadness in response to loss is a perfectly natural part of life. It is as normal as eating and sleeping. It is a necessary part of life. It is inevitable. If we live, we will experience loss. And if we experience loss, we will experience sorrow.

Notice, however, that in this passage of Scripture, grief is interwoven with joy.

> There is a time for everything,
> and a season for every activity under heaven: . . .
>
> a time to kill and a time to heal,
> a time to tear down and a time to build,
> a time to weep and a time to laugh,
> a time to mourn and a time to dance . . .
> a time to embrace and a time to refrain . . .
> a time to love and a time to hate,
> a time for war and a time for peace.
> (Ecclesiastes 3:1–8)

Grief takes time, but grief precedes growth, so it is worth it. Recognize your sadness for what it is. As you progress through your sadness, be aware of the lessons to be learned. Use your sadness for your own growth but don't lodge in it.

THE CONTINUUM OF SADNESS AND DEPRESSION

We like to think of sadness and depression as a continuum. Look at figure 4.1. Notice that there is quite a bit of space between sadness and depression. That is because there is quite a bit of difference between the two. On the left side of the continuum is a mild response to loss. This expression of emotion may be "the blues," as some term it. Or it may be occasional tears. These symptoms are perfectly normal.

Sadness —————————————————————— Depression
Mild   Moderate   Severe
FIGURE 4:1

A greater loss could move someone toward the right on the continuum, to the moderate area. This stage involves a deeper preoccupation with loss and more intense sadness and crying, but it is still a normal response. Whether Jesus was grieving over the death of His friend or grieving His upcoming crucifixion, He was probably in the moderate range of the continuum. His circumstances were severe, but He never lost hope or perspective.

On the far right of the continuum is depression. This stage is a severe response to loss and is more concerning than the other two areas. A person at this end of the continuum experiences deep despair and anguish, a sense of helplessness and hopelessness. In extreme cases, the person has little or no eternal perspective. Instead he experiences only a narrow vision focused mainly on himself and his loss. His life perspectives are distorted and his thoughts are sometimes irrational.

If you have experienced sadness on this end of the continuum, you may have found yourself crying for hours on end and isolating yourself from those who could have supported you. You may have noticed changes in your appetite or sleep patterns. You may have felt physically drained and fatigued, with no motivation to carry out daily responsibilities. Or you may have felt absolutely hopeless—even found yourself thinking about dying or wanting to hurt yourself to avoid the inescapable pain.

But this end of the continuum is *not* God's plan for your life. These are the characteristics of *clinical depression*. If you are facing these symptoms in your infertility grief, or if you have a history of clinical depression or a genetic predisposition to depression, contact your pastor, your physician, and a Christian counselor or psychiatrist—now. You will probably need counseling to pull out of this level of depression. You may also need medication to relieve your symptoms. Ask your counselor for a referral to a Christian psychiatrist, who can evaluate your need for medication, and be sure to follow their recommendations.

SADNESS: SHOCK THE SECOND TIME AROUND

Sadness in regard to infertility grief is shock the second time around. It is the gradual soaking in of the truth, feeling the depth of the sorrow of childlessness, truly experiencing the loss. If you have experienced infertility, you are going to have times of sadness. This is inevitable, it is normal, *and it is OK*. In fact, because infertility for some may be such a long-lasting "cross to bear," it is perfectly normal to expect occasional tears, blues, and sadness throughout your days. Even if you adopt children, you may still experience times of sadness over not having biological children in your home. However, it must be noted that many adoptive parents experience complete fulfillment through the children God has placed in their homes.

Some months will be worse than others. There are common triggers that will bring about your sadness and tears. If you have been in fertility treatment and have been hopeful about the possibility of pregnancy, you are going to be hit with sadness if you begin your menstrual cycle. This sadness may be the kind that moves toward severe depression. Your sorrow will be particularly likely if the fertility treatment was intense, expensive, or your last option. Women who suffer from symptoms of premenstrual syndrome (PMS) are already experiencing hormonal changes that affect moods. Multiply the emotional effects of PMS with the hormonal changes caused by fertility medications and you have a good explanation for the jumble of tears and emotions you feel as you start your cycle.

Holidays may also trigger feelings of sadness and depression. You may be more aware of your loss as you see friends and family with their children at reunions and celebrations. Basically, anything that could have propelled you into shock the first time (as you came out of denial) can retrigger your sorrow or depression in this stage.

Do you ever analyze your infertility? Do you ever wonder, *What if I had done this, or taken that pill, or gone to that doctor, or not taken birth control, or not committed this sin or that sin? What if my husband had not gotten that virus, or if he had always worn boxers, or* . . . The "What ifs?" are endless. Analyzing is normal, but it is not always helpful. Recognize your "What ifs?" for what they are. Then set boundaries and do not let them grow. Though analyzing is normal and to be expected, it can easily push you further than you want to go on the sadness/depression continuum. Analyzing promotes an inward focus that leads to self-pity. If you have already been there, don't beat yourself up over it, but don't go back. Self-pity is a trap and will lead you to depression in record time.

SADNESS AND YOUR MARRIAGE

What has been the effect of your sadness on your marriage? In what ways have you and your spouse dealt with this emotion? Men and women are very different in their expression of emotions, particularly sadness. Women are more likely to talk through their sorrow; men are more likely to bottle it and keep it inside. Women are more likely to want to ask the "What ifs?" Men are more likely to suppress their questions and attempt to move on with life. Society gives women permission to cry while discouraging men's expression of emotions. Because of this, men are more likely to isolate themselves in their sadness. Women are more likely to tell their story of sadness; men are more likely to move on to another subject. Women like to share feelings; men like to find solutions. It is not that the sexes *feel* sadness with any greater or lesser intensity; it's just that they *express* this sadness differently.

Has this difference of expression caused distance in your marriage?

Have you felt your spouse didn't care because he didn't want to talk to you about your loss? Have you felt rejected because he needed to be alone? Have you felt frustrated because he always changes the subject when you bring up infertility? A great deal of marital conflict has occurred over a misunderstanding of feelings. If you are in this stage of grief, you need your spouse's support and understanding. Gently let him know what you need and what you expect. But also remember what he might need and what he expects. Allow your sadness to bring you closer and to a better understanding of one another rather than pull you apart.

THE GENERATION GAP
IN TALKING OPENLY ABOUT SADNESS

Just as the sexes express their emotions differently, so do persons in various generations. Your parents or grandparents may not be willing to talk openly with you about your sorrow over childlessness. In their generation, it was taboo to express emotions openly. Of course, today it is strongly encouraged. Remember, if you don't feel that you are getting what you need from your family, it may be because of a difference in how emotions are expressed. Don't take their silence personally, but make sure you get the support you need from someone who is comfortable with your expression of sadness.

STRATEGIES FOR COPING

Here are some strategies that can help you cope with sadness and depression. Choose those things that fit best for you and get active in helping yourself.

1. *Speak openly about your experiences, both to God and to others.* This is what Jesus, Elijah, Job, and Hannah did. They spoke openly about their feelings. They didn't try to hide the obvious. There is a tremendous sense of relief when we honestly speak our feelings to God and to those who are close to us. But be cautious too. Just as Hannah carefully chose to explain her situation to the priest, we would encourage you to be care-

ful in choosing the person with whom to share your feeling. Another Christian friend is probably your best choice. Speaking our feelings seems to decrease their intensity and control over us. As you are speaking to God in the form of prayer, ask Him to take your burden. With His help, attempt to leave your burden with Him.

2. *Exercise.* It is healthful to get outside and enjoy the sunlight and fresh air. It is also true that God gave us a natural antidepressant that is released when our bodies are active. Plus, doesn't it feel great when you know you are taking care of the temple that God gave you?

3. *Get a proper amount of sleep and eat nutritiously.* Diet can have a significant bearing on a person's emotional and psychological health. Eat more fruits and vegetables and fewer sugars and starches. Remember Elijah? When Elijah was confronted by God after seeking refuge in the cave, an angel of the Lord appeared to him on two different occasions, saying, "Get up and eat" (1 Kings 19:5, 7). God would not have commanded eating if it were not important for Elijah. Nourishment is also important for *you* as you face your time of sadness and disappointment.

4. *Schedule your crying time.* If crying is normal—and it *is*—set aside time for it. Plan to ponder your loss (and nothing else) and cry for thirty minutes a day until you are finished crying. You will be surprised at how few days it will take for you to exhaust your tears and gain a fresh perspective on your loss.

5. *Look expectantly for the maturity that comes with growth.* Praise God for the molding and shaping you have endured through your sadness. This process of maturing is part of God's purpose. During this time of praise, fill your thoughts with the promises of God. Establish a routine for studying the Scriptures. Unlike your need for crying, which will decrease over time, your longing for the Word will increase!

WATER FROM THE ROCK

GOD IS BIGGER THAN YOUR SADNESS

What would happen if you continued in your sadness without taking action? You would move closer to the right side of the continuum into depression (figure 4.1). Or maybe you would revert to the previous grief stage of desperation/panic (chapter 2) in an attempt to find something that will wipe away your sadness. But why allow yourself to become worse if it's not necessary? Instead, invest some energy in working through your sadness so that you can move beyond this stage into the rest of the grief process. You are well over the hump at this point, and there is a great journey ahead. Remember: God is bigger than your sadness. God is stronger than your depression. Press on!

Application Questions

1. *Take a close look at the sadness/depression continuum demonstrated in this chapter. Star and date the place on the continuum you find yourself today. Where would you like to be six months from now?*

2. *If you are feeling sadness or depression, what do you think are the causes? What is the root?*

3. *What specific steps will you take to overcome your sorrow? (Remember, through Christ you are worthy of overcoming.)*

4. *How can you use your experiences with sorrow to minister to someone else?*

5. *Write out at least two Scripture passages that are a source of encour-*

agement to you in times of sadness. Memorize them for easy accessibility. Share them with others.

Victory Verses

"*Come to me, all you who are weary and burdened, and I will give you rest.*"
—MATTHEW 11:28

Cast your cares on the Lord and he will sustain you.
—PSALM 55:22

"*What are you doing here?*"
—1 KINGS 19:9

"*Yet ye have not, because ye ask not.*"
—JAMES 4:2B KJV

FROM HOPE TO ACTION

Decide to do something for someone else
who is struggling in some way.
Take the focus off of your own sorrow
and place it on someone else.
Act on your decision to serve this week.

5

INADEQUACY/GUILT

"What is my purpose now?"

I don't have a child because God knows I wouldn't be a good enough parent."

"If I can't give my spouse a baby, I'm not good enough for him."

"I shouldn't have had the abortion when I was fifteen. I'm being punished, and even though I have asked for forgiveness, I don't deserve to get pregnant."

"I shouldn't have had sex before I was married; I'm being punished for my actions."

"I've done so many wrong things in my life . . . I'm unlovable. No wonder God hasn't given me a child."

"If I just had more faith, I wouldn't grieve over my childlessness."

"I feel guilty about my infertility."

"I feel guilty about my grief."

"I feel guilty about my jealousy."

"I feel guilty for feeling guilty."

Insignificant. Incomplete. Insufficient. Inadequate. Incompetent. Inferior. Worthless! Do these words describe your view of yourself? Have you ever felt completely unacceptable? If you have placed your worth and value in becoming a mother, and then faced the trial of infertility, it's certain that you've felt pretty low. Perhaps you can identify with the following testimony.

> After a series of failed fertility endeavors, I felt utterly despicable. I recorded in my journal feelings of sadness and loneliness. I felt ugly, defective, and undesirable. I was so caught up in my endeavor for a child that it became my identity. When that endeavor failed, I—along with my identity—was crushed.
>
> The deeper I sank into my worthlessness, the more intensely I began to compare myself to others. The more I compared, the more worthless I felt—and the more jealous.

You can imagine what this cycle and its destructiveness feels like. Look with us in this chapter as we examine varying degrees of feelings of inadequacy and guilt as well as specific, biblical strategies for moving beyond this stage of grief. Together, let's learn the truth about who we are and what our identity is.

DISTORTION OF TRUTH

What characterizes this stage of inadequacy and guilt? *Distortion of truth.* It is a belief in a distorted version of yourself and your situation. It is blaming yourself for your shattered dreams. It is holding yourself captive to a situation only God can control—for only God can handle a God-sized situation. Be aware that Satan thrives on a distortion of the truth (John 8:44). If you have struggled with thoughts that you are insignificant, incomplete, insufficient, inadequate, incompetent, inferior, or worthless, you have been believing a lie. You have faced a war against the Enemy. He's found a weak spot, and he wants to take advantage of it.

CONDITIONS THAT AFFECT YOUR
FEELINGS OF INADEQUACY AND GUILT

As we've said, this stage affects its victims in varying degrees. What determines how severely you will experience inadequacy or guilt? Five conditions will affect whether you will even *pass* through this stage, and if so, to what depth.

1. *Your relationship with God.* Why is this relationship so important? Because the only way to get through life and not feel inadequate is to have your identity soaked in Christ, for He understands you (Hebrews 4:15–16). If a relationship with God is a struggle for you, you will more easily struggle with feelings of inadequacy. If you are distant from God, you probably feel worthless and useless. If you have never accepted Christ as your Savior, you do not know the power of His healing. When our focus is on Him, we are better able to appreciate and love ourselves.

If you already have a close walk with your Savior, then you may be better able to see yourself through His eyes as the beautiful, acceptable being He created you to be. Your identity will rest in the reality that you *are* His child, not in your ability to *carry* a child. If you reach the point where you experience true contentment in your spiritual life, you will no longer experience feelings of inadequacy, for contentment and a sense of inadequacy cannot co-exist. Be patient. This transformation takes time.

2. *Your relationship with your spouse.* The depth to which you experience this stage will be affected by your relationship with your spouse. The people we spend our time with influence the way we view our world and ourselves. If your spouse loves you unconditionally and emotionally supports you through your infertility trial, you are more likely to pass through this stage with ease. Be sure to praise God for your loving spouse.

But if your spouse beats you down with verbal insults, you may struggle to keep your head above water. If this is your situation, you are going to have to make a choice. You must ask yourself, *Whom am I going to believe? The person who is telling me I am worthless and incomplete, or my Creator, who assures me that I am thoughtfully and perfectly created in His very own image?* (Psalm 139; Jeremiah 1:5). Choosing to believe God doesn't mean that you have to create a conflict with your spouse; it means that you should live your life acknowledging to yourself the truth about who you really are. As you discover your transformed identity and completeness in Christ, you will be better able to rise above your situation.

3. *Your support system.* This system can include friends, family, church members, and colleagues. Do you have friends with whom you can talk? Friends to whom you can go when you feel unacceptable? Friends who understand your loss? Do you have a special friend who can comfort you with the comfort she's received from God (2 Corinthians 1:4)? If you already have this support system, put it to use. If not, pray diligently that God will provide one. You need people who love you and can confirm your great worth.

4. *Your use of your spiritual gift(s).* Did you know that when you were saved, the Holy Spirit gave you a spiritual gift (or gifts)? The fourth chapter of Ephesians and the twelfth chapter of the first letter of Paul to the Corinthians discuss these special gifts given to all believers. Do you know what your gift is? Perhaps it is mercy; or maybe it is hospitality. Perhaps it is evangelism or teaching or administration. There are many possibilities, because God made you *uniquely* in His image. If you are uncertain about what your spiritual gift is, see your pastor for assistance. Ask him to pray with you that God will reveal your gift or gifts to you. Pray that He will open doors of opportunity for you to use those gifts.

Can you imagine the impact on your sense of self if you were fully exercising your spiritual gift? Can you envision the blessings you would not only *receive* but *bestow* upon others? How could you possibly feel useless knowing that God is using you to fulfill His purposes?

5. *A childhood history of abuse.* If you have experienced verbal abuse, you may struggle over some of the lies told to you. You may mentally repeat those accusations as though they were videotaped. If you grew up feeling inadequate and not valuable, your experience with infertility may have confirmed your suspicions. *Do not allow the wounds of the past*

to continue to dictate your life. You are valuable. You are complete. You are significant. God has a wonderful purpose for your life. If a history of abuse plagues you and complicates your infertility grief, please seek help for it now. You do not have to continue living your life in the darkness of the past.

GETTING OUT OF THE CYCLE OF INADEQUACY

If you meet one or all of these conditions, you may already be familiar with what can happen next. When you struggle with inadequacy, you are vulnerable to a vicious cycle. Think about it. If you really feel that you are defective or lacking, then you also feel that you don't deserve good things from life. That causes you to settle for less than God's best—because you don't think you are worthy of God's best. You may even begin to make a series of bad choices. Those bad choices confirm what you think about yourself—that you are pathetic and unacceptable. Pretty soon you may begin putting yourself down in front of others. You may even begin labeling yourself as infertile, rather than as a beautiful child of God. Your struggle, your grief, and your loss become your identity.

What do you do to avoid this stage? Or, if you are already in the depths of this cycle, how do you get out? The answer is easy to remember but difficult to implement. *Your adequacy must come from God.* This recognition is the only stable, sufficient solution. Your adequacy cannot come from your ability to conceive, your ability to carry full term, or your ability to discipline children. Nor can it come from your spouse's approval, your career success, or your excellence in comparison to other people. We're reminded of the comforting words of Paul in 2 Corinthians 3:5: "Not that we are competent in ourselves to claim anything for ourselves; but our competence comes from God." What a burden lifted! Our significance is not in our fertility but in Christ. What's more significant than that?

When our adequacy is rooted in Christ, we will feel the effects. When we are beaten down by a sense of guilt, we can determine the source and see if there is any sin about us. If there is, we can move forward by asking forgiveness. When we see others who are doing better than we, we can be released from comparisons. When people are critical of us, we don't have to let them dictate our self-worth, even if those people are important to us. We don't have to be held captive by obstacles but can go to the One who gives "liberty to the captives" (Isaiah 61:1 KJV). "You, my brothers, were called to be free" (Galatians 5:13). Having found this freedom, you have the opportunity to be held eternally captive by God, the lover of your soul. And captivity in God is total freedom.

LEARNING TO BE CONTENT

Again, it's impossible to have feelings of inadequacy and feelings of contentment at the same time. When our adequacy is in Christ, we have the opportunity to experience true contentment. The apostle Paul referred to contentment as something he had to learn (Philippians 4:11–13). This statement implies that contentment did not come naturally for him. Imagine the struggle he must have faced as he was being transformed from Saul, the persecutor of Christians (Acts 8:1–3), to Paul the apostle (Acts 9:1–9; 15:12–26; 2 Timothy 1:11). How easily he could have been plagued with guilt over his past. Yet Paul learned to place his self-worth in his willingness to be used as a vessel for Christ. He chose to forget his past and focus on his future with God (Philippians 3:13; compare Acts 8:1–3). "I have been crucified with Christ and I no longer live," he said (Galatians 2:20). His ultimate transformation was in realizing that his old self was dead. He became truly alive and valuable through his new relationship with Christ. All of his guilt and inadequacy died with his old self, freeing his new self to be used in a mighty way.

Even as Paul continued in his ministry, his sufferings could have robbed him of contentment. From his jail bed, he could have said, "What is happening to me is horrible and paralyzing. This persecution is awful. I can't believe it." Instead, he said that his trial served to further the gospel (Philippians 1:12). He gained peace through embracing his suffering and strength through embracing his weakness (2 Corinthians 12:9–10). He had an eternal perspective that granted him contentment. This perspective could have only been the result of a close relationship with his Creator.

INADEQUACY VS. HUMILITY

Paul knew the difference between inadequacy and humility. He lessened himself so that Christ could be exalted through him. This lessening could be mistaken for inadequacy, but it's certain that Paul felt anything but inadequate. Humility is meekness and modesty. It is not undue self-depreciation. We are reminded in James 4:10 and 1 Peter 5:6 that in our humility, Christ will lift us up. We must trust that Christ will fill the void and complete our souls. If we humbly give ourselves to Christ—barrenness and all—He will complete and empower us. His grace is sufficient for you. His power is made perfect in your weakness; boast in your weakness so that God's power will work through you (2 Corinthians 12:9–10).

If motherhood is your only identity, you are missing out on something very important: A mother is not significant because she is a *mother* but because she is a *child*. The fact that she is a child of God makes her valuable. There is no favoritism with God (Ephesians 6:9). God does not love you less because of your infertility. If you are a child of God, you are sufficient. You are adequate. You are competent. You are complete. You are whole. You are worthy. You are valued. You are useful. You are accepted. You are loved. *Forget the past.* Don't focus on your struggle but on the race ahead (Philippians 3:13–14). Press on!

Application Questions

1. *What are the distorted thoughts you often repeat to yourself? Write them down. Do these phrases lead you to feel complete or inadequate? Compare these thoughts with the instructions of Philippians 4:8, which says, "Whatever is true, whatever is honorable, whatever is just, whatever is pure, whatever is pleasing, whatever is commendable, if*

there is any excellence and if there is anything worthy of praise, think about these things" *(NRSV). What is the truth for each of the distorted thoughts you recorded? (Write out the truth beside each distorted thought.)*

2. *Review the five conditions that affect the degree to which you may experience this stage. Which conditions apply to you? How have they impacted your feelings of inadequacy or guilt through your infertility grief?*

3. *What bad choices have you made as a result of feeling inadequate? If you are a Christian, do you now know that you are worthy of God's best?*

4. *If you were honest, in what would you say you place your identity? In your infertility, your appearance, your career, your spouse, your accomplishments, your relationship with Christ? Do your answers add to feelings of inadequacy or contentment?*

Victory Verses

But who are you, O man, to talk back to God?
Shall what is formed say to him who formed it,
"Why did you make me like this?"
—ROMANS 9:20

Therefore, there is now no condemnation
for those who are in Christ Jesus.
—ROMANS 8:1

*And be not conformed to this world, but be ye transformed by
the renewing of your mind, that ye may prove what is
that good, and acceptable, and perfect, will of God.*
—ROMANS 12:2 KJV

*For you created my inmost being; you knit me
together in my mother's womb. I praise you because
I am fearfully and wonderfully made.*
—PSALM 139:13–14

*Forgetting what is behind and straining toward what is
ahead, I press on toward the goal to win the prize for which
God has called me heavenward in Christ Jesus.*
—PHILIPPIANS 3:13–14

Ye shall know the truth, and the truth shall make you free.
—JOHN 8:32 KJV

*But now he has reconciled you by Christ's physical
body through death to present you holy in his sight,
without blemish and free from accusation.*
—COLOSSIANS 1:22

*"[Satan] was a murderer from the beginning,
not holding to the truth, for there is no truth in him.
When he lies, he speaks his native language,
for he is a liar and the father of lies."*
—JOHN 8:44

FROM HOPE TO ACTION

Write a letter to God. Thank Him and praise Him for His forgiveness of you. Praise Christ for His suffering on your behalf. Praise Him for His glory. Remember, if God's forgiveness of you is sufficient for Him, shouldn't it be sufficient for you?

6

HOPE/PEACE

"I'm OK."

Two days before we started to write this chapter, on September 11, 2001, terrorists brought death to thousands of innocent Americans by hijacking commercial jets and turning them into missiles aimed at the World Trade Center Towers in New York and the Pentagon in Washington, D.C. As we saw these terrible events unfold on television, we experienced a deep need for hope and peace.

How do we find hope in the midst of this tragedy? Can anything good come from our despair? Can healing occur? Absolutely! America has the opportunity to *choose* to hope—in the only One who *is* hope! In Psalm 121, a question is proposed and an answer provided: "I lift up my eyes to the hills—where does my help come from? My help comes from the LORD, the Maker of heaven and earth" (vv. 1–2). Our Creator, our "keeper," is our hope. It is by dwelling in His "shelter" that we are able to live in peace (Psalm 91).

What about our trial of infertility? Is hope to be found in this crisis too? Stay with us as we take a closer look at how to be hopeful and peaceful in the midst of difficult circumstances.

A New Mind-set

Notice the difference in these two journal entries:

January 1

As this journal seemed to start as an infertility journal, I guess I need to address our current status: NOTHING! However, God has promised a peace beyond our understanding if we place our faith in Him, and I praise God for the peace I have (Philippians 4:7). I do yearn for a child, but become more and more convinced each day of the sovereignty of God. I don't need to worry about what the future holds for me, but embrace each day with confidence that God knows what will happen and already has His hand in my future. Yet, there is this instinctual desire to experience the gift of birth and the selfish desire to look into the eyes of a child that resembles my husband and me. Lord, help me to let go of the desires that depress me and hinder my relationship with you. Help me to cling to the desires of your heart . . . the desires that give me peace.

March 21

God, forgive me of my poor attitude and lusting over what I do not have. Help me to be satisfied in mind and *spirit. I want to feel satisfied so that I can be grateful. Nothing in my circumstance needs to change to make that happen, and I'm not asking for a change in order to be satisfied. I'm asking for a pure heart . . . a changed heart . . . a grateful, satisfied heart.*

Wow, what a relief! Now there's a transition. Notice that nothing has changed about the circumstance of infertility, yet there is a definite difference in *mind-set* in the two journal entries. Have you sometimes felt incapable of experiencing hope or peace? No doubt you have! But you were created *fully* capable of experiencing the kind of peace that surpasses all circumstances and all understanding (Philippians 4:7). Galatians 5:22 lists peace as a fruit of the Spirit. If you are a Christian, you have access to peace. God can replace the tears of all of your circumstances with hope. Join us as we take a look at this stage of grief, a stage characterized by replacing the mourning of previous stages with hope and purpose (Isaiah 61). This stage brings new energy and a fresh look at the future.

A FOCUS ON THE FUTURE

What is the difference between this stage and those before it? The earlier stages focused on the past or the present. This stage focuses on the future—on a workable, acceptable future. If you are in this stage, your *situation* has probably not changed at all. You may still be childless. You may be pursuing treatment or adoption options. You may have ceased all efforts as you take a respite from the strain of the "baby quest." Or you may have decided that you are content without children. The point is, it is not your situation that has spurred your entrance into this stage of grief. It is your *focus* that has allowed you to progress. Living in the knowledge of the facts of your infertility, you can still say, "I'm OK. There is a future for me."

Hope certainly doesn't mean that we know what our future holds. The Scriptures remind us that "hope that is seen is no hope at all" (Romans

8:24). Hope means that we have faith in *whatever* our futures hold. And what does God have to say about our future? "'For I know the plans I have for you,' declares the LORD, 'plans to prosper you and not to harm you, plans to give you hope and a future'" (Jeremiah 29:11). God has already told us that He has chosen for us a life of hope and peace. God does not focus on a perishing past but on a plentiful future.

PREREQUISITES TO HOPE

What is hope, and how do you get it? What is peace, and where is it to be found? In terms of our infertility grief, *hope* should be used as a noun. Therefore, it is a possession available to you *right now*. Think of the word *hopeless*. It denotes the lack of a solution and the lack of a future. *Hope* is the exact opposite—it denotes confidence in a satisfying future. This confidence results in peace.

There are *prerequisites* to hope. Hope is not possible without "something else" first.

1. *First of all, that "something else" is a relationship with and faith in Jesus Christ.* Our salvation—our repentance and Jesus' forgiveness—is the first step to hope. Our salvation leads to a transformation of ourselves and a desire to seek God's will, as explained in His Word. Our hope must come from God and His Word (Psalms 62:5; 130:5). But how do we get this hope from His Word? Take a look at the next prerequisite for the answer.

2. *The second prerequisite for hope is abiding in God's Word and dwelling in His presence through prayer (Psalm 91:1).* The King James Version of Psalm 91:1 describes His presence as a "secret place." God's presence is a safe shelter of which we cannot be robbed. It is a "refuge," a refuge of hope (v. 9). God's presence is eternally available for our dwelling. The term *dwelling* indicates that we are to set up residence, or live, there. Psalm 91:9 says that if we make the Lord our dwelling, He will become our refuge.

As Christians, we have the opportunity to find harbor in this safe haven. We are instructed to bring our needs to God; He will guard our hearts and minds and give us peace (Philippians 4:6–7). Why would we not choose to dwell in this place of comfort? Why would we not want to live in this place of hope and peace? Our faith can translate our hopeless circumstances and pasts into hopeful, peace-filled futures.

3. *The third prerequisite for hope is accepting God's sovereignty.* This step is understanding and believing that God has the desire and the ability to move you from where you are to a place of purpose and restoration, the place He calls "a hope and a future" (Jeremiah 29:11). God's curative power is unlimited and undisputed. He has the power to heal your body and your grief. God is 100 percent sovereign, 100 percent supreme, 100 percent successful. He sent a 100 percent Savior to deliver us. He is the complete soul satisfier.

If you have experienced the trial of infertility and have made it to this stage, you can look back over some difficult times. Be assured, the time it took to get to this stage was valuable. This time in your life was a training ground that enabled you to develop strength and endurance. Congratulations for fighting the fight and keeping the faith. We know it has not been an easy battle. God has promised to provide good for those of us who love Him (Romans 8:28). We know that you are about to experience some of that good as a reward for placing your faith in Christ in the midst of your trial.

THE SUFFERING THAT LEADS TO HOPE

We don't move from difficulty to hope in one just one step. There is a progression and a pattern, as Romans 5:3–5 (RSV) shows.

We rejoice in our sufferings, knowing that suffering produces endurance, and endurance produces character, and character produces hope, and hope does not disappoint us, because God's love has been poured into our hearts through the Holy Spirit that has been given to us.

Suffering, endurance, character, hope. The pattern begins with difficulty and ends with a hope that will not let us down. God has never told us we would always have it easy. In fact, He forewarned us, "In the world ye shall have tribulation: but be of good cheer; I have overcome the world" (John 16:33 KJV).

The Scriptures describe Jesus as "a man of sorrows, and acquainted with grief" (Isaiah 53:3 KJV). He was familiar with suffering. God allowed His only Son to suffer out of His desire to expand His kingdom with His children. God knew that the result would be worth the price. He knew He would not be disappointed (vv. 10–12). Jesus' desire to bring children into the heavenly kingdom placed on Him suffering no other person has or ever will experience (Psalm 22:1–18; Isaiah 52:14, 53:1–12; Hebrews 2:10). He bore the sins of the entire world in His suffering (Galatians 3:13) and fulfilled the heavenly Father's desire to offer salvation to anyone who would believe and accept Him (John 3:16–18).

Do you see the resemblance to your trial of infertility? God has allowed you to experience the suffering that gradually leads to the hope that "does not disappoint" (Romans 5:5). We can overcome this suffering because He has already overcome our tribulations. In Romans 5:2, we are reminded to "rejoice" in this "hope of the glory of God." We can rejoice because we are "joint-heirs with Christ" (Romans 8:17 KJV).

THE REWARDS OF HOPE AND PEACE

What an honor to have the opportunity to suffer alongside our Savior! Furthermore, our present sufferings are incomparable to the "glory which shall be revealed in us" (Romans 8:18 KJV). You see, one of the effects of this stage of hope is that you are able to rejoice regardless of your suffering, because God has used it to mold you into a hope-filled, peace-filled child. Praise God, for He has assured you that He will not fail you! Praise God, for He has used your suffering to produce something good.

There are many other wonderful rewards of experiencing hope and peace. As you look back to the previous stages of grief, you may feel stuck and sluggish or stressed and strained. In contrast, hope promotes useful activity. Hope does not hinder; it allows us to move on with life. Hope allows us to concentrate on something other than our trial. Hope allows us to feel purposeful again. It allows us to rest, relax, settle ourselves, and really begin to live again.

Many women who experience infertility feel that their bodies are dead, incapable of bearing life. This feeling of a lack of purpose traps many. Yet, the Scriptures encourage us: "A heart at peace gives life to the body" (Proverbs 14:30). Though your body may not produce the life of a child, the life God has given you is tremendously valuable to Him. A reward of hope is life where we once thought there was deadness.

HANNAH

In chapter 4, we discussed the experience of Hannah, recorded in 1 Samuel 1:1–2:10. We hope you took the opportunity to do further study of Hannah at that time. However, if you did not, we encourage you to do so now. You see, we witnessed Hannah experiencing the depths of infertility grief, but we are able to also witness a powerful transition in her grief. As Hannah focused on God and placed her faith in Him, she found hope and strength. Her faith within caused her outward countenance to change. She began eating again, continued her daily activities, and gained victory over her depression. She sought God through her emotional storm of infertility as well as the scorn of a society who failed to accept her. She walked with grace.

Hannah did not pray for God to calm her *storm;* she prayed for God to calm *her.* In return, God delivered her from depression, anger, and a sense of inadequacy. Her hope in God brought healing to her emotional wounds and prepared her to rejoice in His presence.

HOPE, PEACE, AND PRAISE

Hope and peace prepare us to praise. We praise *despite* our circumstances. We praise *during* our circumstances. We praise *because* of our circumstances. Take a look at Psalm 71. The psalmist is living with trouble, attack, calamity, and accusation. But what do we see him doing? He goes to God in prayer. He dwells in the presence of God and praises Him. He faithfully proclaims his assurance that the One who gave him life would restore it. He understands God's plan to prosper him and praises God because he is confident that God will be faithful to His plan. What an example to us!

As we face the complex challenge of childlessness, we can come into the presence of God in prayer with praises. For what can you praise God? Will you praise Him for His plans to give you hope? Will you accept His desires for a hope-filled future? A change will occur in you when you begin to praise Him. Peace will be the result of this new attitude. This act of praise will be a springboard to the healing that will prepare you to move to the final stage of grief. This last stage is true *water from the rock*. Let's look expectantly toward it, anxiously awaiting the newfound freedom God eagerly desires to bestow upon all of us.

Application Questions

1. *Think of a life trial from the past that you have overcome. How did you find hope again? What can this experience teach you about finding hope and peace in your trial of infertility?*

2. *What obstacles are preventing you from experiencing hope? What if you never choose to hope?*

3. *For what do you have reason to praise God, even as you face your trial of infertility? (Realize that this praise is a necessary catalyst for complete healing.)*

4. *What does God desire for your life? Will you accept the abundant, hope-filled life He has planned for you?*

Victory Verses

"Peace I leave with you; my peace I give to you.
I do not give to you as the world gives. Do not let
your hearts be troubled, and do not be afraid."
—JOHN 14:27

Do not be anxious about anything, but in everything, by prayer
and petition, with thanksgiving, present your requests to God.
And the peace of God, which transcends all understanding, will
guard your hearts and your minds in Christ Jesus.
—PHILIPPIANS 4:6–7

Draw near to God and He will draw near to you.
—JAMES 4:8 NKJV

Thou wilt keep him in perfect peace, whose mind is stayed on
thee: because he trusteth in thee.
—ISAIAH 26:3 KJV

Yet you are enthroned as the Holy One; you are the praise of Israel.
—PSALM 22:3

FROM HOPE TO ACTION

Write a song of praise to God for the good
that has come out of your suffering.
Use Scripture verses of hope.

7

RECONCILIATION/
INTEGRATION

"May your will be done."

In John 15:1–8 Jesus gives believers a description of true healing.

"I am the true vine, and My Father is the vinedresser. Every branch in Me that does not bear fruit He takes away; and every branch that bears fruit He prunes, that it may bear more fruit. You are already clean because of the word which I have spoken to you. Abide in Me, and I in you. As the branch cannot bear fruit of itself, unless it abides in the vine, neither can you, unless you abide in Me. I am the vine, you are the branches. He who abides in Me, and I in him, bears much fruit; for without Me you can do nothing. If anyone does not abide in Me, he is cast out as a branch and is withered; and they gather them and throw them into the fire, and they are burned. If you abide in Me, and My words abide in you,

you will ask what you desire, and it shall be done for you. By this My Father is glorified, that you bear much fruit; so you will be My disciples." (NKJV)

Why do we say this passage is about healing? We say so because it describes the process and result of healing. Jesus is the vine. Think of a grapevine. What is its purpose? The vine is the source of life, strength, nutrition, and shape for the plant. Without the vine, the plant would not exist or bear fruit.

The heavenly Father is the vinedresser. What does a vinedresser do? He cares for the vine and the branches and does what is necessary for the vineyard to produce a good crop. He makes the final call and sees to the details of life.

We are the branches. Our job is to produce good and abundant fruit. If we are to grow this fruit, we must abide in (rest in and stay connected with) the vine and be cooperative with the work of the vinedresser. We need to be obedient to Him.

The health of the vineyard depends on the branches staying connected to the vine and yielding to the work of the vinedresser. We are introduced in this Scripture passage to the organization and arrangement of authority. In times of suffering, isn't it comforting to know that our Father above is in control?

THE VINE, THE VINEDRESSER, AND OUR INFERTILITY

So what does this Scripture passage have to do with our trial of infertility? It has to do with what is produced spiritually through our trials. If you are a Christian, you are a branch. If you have seen a grapevine lately, you have noticed that some branches produce hundreds of grapes, whereas others are barren. The branches that are barren eventually become brittle and fall off. So it is with us. Branches can do nothing apart from the vine on which they grow. If we are not abiding in the vine, we will not be able to produce spiritual fruit and will be useless to the vine.

In chapter 6, we talked about the fruit of the Spirit, which Christ develops within us (Galatians 5:22–23). In this stage of *reconciliation and integration,* the inward fruit of the Spirit begins to produce outward fruit. As your inward peace develops, it begins to spill over. This spilling over is a reflection of the love of Christ to people everywhere. This fruit makes an impact on the kingdom of God. Whether you have children or not, you are called to be a fruitful branch. John 15:16 says, "You did not choose Me, but I chose you and appointed you that you should go and bear fruit, and that your fruit should remain" (NKJV). If you are a child of God, you are incredibly special. You are a chosen branch called to bear specific fruit that only you can bear. The fruit you are chosen to bear may or may not be physical life, but it will certainly be spiritual life.

PRUNING

What determines whether a branch will produce fruit? What determines whether a Christian will produce spiritual fruit? You're not going to like the answer. Pruning. Pruning is the process by which the vinedresser molds and shapes the branch into what He desires it to be. It is only by pruning that more fruit can be produced. The pruner has to have a "big picture" perspective. He has to know that the cutting away will lead to a desired future and is worth the final product. Pruning determines the quantity and quality of the fruit produced. The good news for you, dear friend, is that if you have made it to this stage of infertility grief, you have experienced a great deal of pruning already.

INTEGRATION

Every stage of grief described so far in this book has been a demonstration of the pruning you have endured. The best news of all is the assurance that your pruning will not be in vain as long as you continue to remain and abide in the One who desires goodness and purpose for you. If you continue to abide, fruit will be produced from your suffering (John 15:5–10). What more comforting thought could you ask for? When we persevere and are willing to integrate our suffering and grief into the rest of our lives, God promises to bring forth life from our barrenness. This integration is true reconciliation and healing of grief.

> Now all things are of God, who has reconciled us to Himself through Jesus Christ, and has given us the ministry of reconciliation. . . . Now then, we are ambassadors for Christ, as though God were pleading through us: we implore you on Christ's behalf, be reconciled to God. For He made Him who knew no sin to be sin for us, that we might become the righteousness of God in Him. (2 Corinthians 5:18, 20–21 NKJV)

Do you realize the message of this Scripture passage? You have a ministry. You are an ambassador through which God makes His appeal to the world. You are a messenger of God, a representative. You have been given the ministry of reconciliation and are called to be a vessel God can use to reconcile the world to Himself. Talk about healing! Talk about purpose! You are *not* inadequate. You have a ministry to complete. Your trial of infertility is not a hindrance; it is a powerful addition to your ministry. Will you allow God to use it? Will you allow Him to draw purpose from your suffering? This recognition of *using* your trial rather than *wasting* it is what integration is all about. It is incorporating your grief into your ministry, all for the glory of God. And our God is worthy of receiving this glory.

DEBORAH

When we think about someone in the Bible who carried out a ministry of reconciliation, we think about Deborah. If you have ever read the book of Judges, you probably remember seeing her story (Judges 4–5). Perhaps you remember her as a wise judge and fearless warrior. Maybe you wonder why we would even bring her up. "What does she have in common with me?" We think the better question is, "How can I have *more* in common with Deborah?" You see, there is no indication in Scripture that Deborah was a natural mother, *but she never allowed the grief of childlessness to imprison her or prevent her from accomplishing God's will in her life.* She had the big picture and an eternal perspective on life. She was a woman full of motherly characteristics which she used to become a mother not just to one or two, but to an entire nation (Judges 5:7). She carried out *a ministry of reconciliation.*

Nurture and Support from Her Husband

Deborah had what was necessary to be a great mother, and in using those gifts she touched thousands of lives. One of the things we learn about Deborah is that she was the wife of Lappidoth. Though we are given very little information about their marriage, we are inclined to believe this was a strong marriage whose focus was on God. It would have been impossible for Deborah to provide the nurture and support to others as she did without receiving the same from her husband. We believe her marriage relationship was a priority in her life and played a vital role in her leadership and "mothering" of Israel. Her marriage relationship must have been a tremendous support to her ministry.

The Ability to Motivate

Another gift Deborah possessed that allowed her to be an effective "mother" to Israel was her ability to motivate. She drew the Israelites away from their fear, gave them enthusiasm to fight even against the odds, and encouraged them to hope for a better future. Despite the fact that her army had only a tenth the manpower of her enemy, she inspired the Israelites to fight, and their victory became a testimony to her faith and perseverance. As a "spiritual mother," she was able to help her "children" fight their enemies. Can you imagine the outcome for Israel if she had not allowed God to make use of the motherly characteristics she possessed? She understood that God's use of her gifts might be different from conventional ones.

The Ability to Mediate

A skill absolutely necessary for mothers is mediation. How often do we see siblings fight and bicker? Likewise, the society of her time thought to go to Deborah when they needed resolution for disagreements, for she was a source of strength and safety. They apparently had confidence in her godly wisdom and advice. Deborah had to provide mediation not just to a few people but to an entire nation. She was so gifted in this area that a tree was named in her honor, "the Palm of Deborah" (Judges 4:5). To understand the significance of this distinction, it would be like a highway being named after a prominent leader in our society. A modern day example is the Billy Graham Parkway in Charlotte, North Carolina. Deborah's spiritual mothering was known to more than just a few.

A Strong Walk with God

The most important characteristic for a mother to have is a strong walk with God. Despite all the other wonderful characteristics of Deborah, the ones that really set her apart were her focus on God, ability to provide spiritual guidance to others, and humility. She gave God the credit for her blessings and taught a nation of people to do the same. Deborah obeyed God's commands in her role as a judge. She was a mother to Israel because she had tremendous faith and because she taught others how to walk in a closer relationship with God. She was a fruitful branch that gained its strength from the heavenly vine.

BEING A SPIRITUAL MOTHER

If you are without children and desire to be a mother, ask God for the desires of your heart. But if He doesn't give you a natural child, look around—perhaps He's preparing you to be a spiritual mother. If so, will you continue to be imprisoned by your grief, or will you allow yourself to be freed by the ministry opportunities God has set before you? We encourage you to choose freedom. Like Deborah, you are called to bear fruit. Allow God to raise you above your grief as He produces this fruit through you.

What would have happened if Deborah had not been obedient? What if she had rejected the calling of the ministry of reconciliation? According to the Scriptures, she would have been considered useless to the king-dom of God. A branch that refuses to seek nourishment from the vine withers away and serves no purpose (John 15:4–6). A branch that refuses to depend on the vine is left incomplete and unfulfilled. In contrast, a branch that obeys and abides in the vine is rewarded with fullness of joy (vv. 10–11). Thank God Deborah had vision and hope. Thank God she had an eternal perspective. She had an incredible purpose, and so do you. Will you choose to exercise it or waste it?

THE REWARDS OF OBEDIENCE

We have challenged you to be obedient as a fruitful branch. What are the rewards of this obedience? They are greater than you can imagine.

A Transformed and Altered Identity

According to Scripture, one of the rewards for this obedience is a transformed and altered identity. John 15:15 teaches us that if we do what God has commanded of us, He no longer calls us servants, "because the servant does not know what his master is doing" (NRSV). Instead, He says, "I have called you friends, because I have made known to you everything that I have heard from my Father" (NRSV). In other words, not only do we have the privilege of better understanding His ways and His charac-ter, but we also have the privilege of being referred to by Him as friends. We become partners with Christ our Savior and are united with Him and share in His sufferings. We have an intimate relationship with Him. We can't think of a reward greater than that.

The Secret of Contentment

Yet God doesn't stop there. He gives us other rewards for our obe-dience in allowing Him to use us as vessels. A second reward for our obedience is the gift of the "secret" of contentment. In the book of Philippians, we have the opportunity to chart Paul as he experiences heal-ing. "I have learned to be content with whatever I have. I know what it is to have little, and I know what it is to have plenty. In any and all circumstances I have learned the secret of being well-fed and of going hungry, of having plenty and of being in need" (Philippians 4:11–12 NRSV). Paul had learned that it is not the circumstance that determines contentment but the intimate relationship with God. Yes, you can have contentment and peace in the midst of your childlessness, because God's purposes are greater than your loss.

Spiritual Maturity

A third reward for this obedience is spiritual maturity. Taking our grief to Christ and asking Him to use it for His purposes gives us an eternal perspective to our suffering. This perspective allows us to see a hopeful view beyond our immediate circumstance. God also provides us wisdom and guidance during our grief. In fact, James 1:5 reminds us that if we are lacking in wisdom, we should ask God, "who gives generously to all without finding fault, and it will be given to [you]."

God does not desire to keep us in the dark during our grief. He is Light, and He desires to bring light and understanding to us if we are willing to come before Him in prayer and ask. The Scriptures also remind us that our testing produces endurance, which is a sign of maturity. James challenges us: "Perseverance must finish its work so that you may be mature and complete, not lacking anything" (James 1:4). If you have felt incomplete or inadequate during your trial of infertility, look up, because your endurance brings completion. You are complete and fulfilled because you have been a faithful branch, producing eternal fruits.

A Lack of Fear

Last, God gives us a fourth encouragement through His revelation to John. He tells us not to fear during our grief. "Do not be afraid of what you are about to suffer. I tell you, the devil will put some of you in prison to test you, and you will suffer persecution for ten days. Be faithful even to the point of death, and I will give you the crown of life" (Revelation 2:10). You may feel imprisoned by your grief over childlessness, but do not give up. God has promised an *eternal* reward for your faithfulness in suffering.

Dying to Ourselves

Our ultimate healing comes from the life that is produced through our relationship with God, whether we have no children or are the mother of many. Regardless of your circumstance, *you must die to yourself in order to experience this life.* This way of life means dying to your circumstances and trusting that the vinedresser is the expert. He knows what to do with the branch to produce life.

The Scriptures remind us of this thought many times. Jesus instructed His followers to deny themselves, take up their cross, and follow Him (Mark 8:34). Perhaps your "cross" is your infertility. Are you willing to "take it up" and follow Jesus? In the book of Galatians, Paul describes his new identity in Christ: "I have been crucified with Christ and I no longer live, but Christ lives in me. The life I live in the body, I live by faith in the Son of God, who loved me and gave himself for me" (2:20).

God's pruning of Paul allowed the apostle to recognize the significance of the cross and Christ's death for him. He no longer lived in constant awareness of his own suffering and struggle; rather, Christ lived in him, giving him the strength and eternal perspective that has impacted generations. Paul understood the concept of our decreasing and Christ's increasing (John 3:30). He understood that if the branch does not die to the authority of the vine, its suffering is useless. We pray that you have come to this same understanding. Don't allow your suffering to be wasted. Your suffering and grief do not have to be in vain. Don't waste your pruning. You have an opportunity to witness something beautiful being produced out of your pain.

Free to Love Others

Once we are prepared to bear fruit, we can complete the greatest commandment we were given, *to love one another* (John 13:34; 1 John 4:7). Reach out to those around you. Care for the women around you who are struggling. Love the women around you who are also facing infertility. Serve those who are in any circumstance, whether they be single, widowed, or a mother to many. Through this expression of your love to others, God is glorified (Matthew 7:20; Luke 6:43–45).

Remember, we are not our own but were "bought at a price" (1 Corinthians 6:19–20). Our grief is not about us; it is about Him. We were created to love and glorify Him, whether in joy or grief. As we reach out to others, God brings us comfort through His Holy Spirit. He promised that He would not leave us comfortless (John 14:16–18 KJV). The more we focus on Him rather than on our suffering, the more comfort we are allowed to receive and the more we are allowed to give.

TRUE HEALING AND RECONCILIATION

In this chapter, we have talked about the final stage of infertility grief. This stage should be your goal. This stage is true healing and reconciliation, because it is true eternal understanding. It is true fellowship with God and others. It is true purpose. It is life. As this healing transformation takes place, you will be lifted from your burdens. You will be able to *integrate* your grief into your life, rather than allowing your grief to *dictate* your life. At this point freedom is gained. This stage is where your ashes become beauty, your mourning becomes joy, your heaviness becomes praise, and the captive is set free (Isaiah 61:1–3).

Reconciliation is acceptance of God's will for you, the restoration of who you were intended to be in Christ Jesus. Romans 5:10; 2 Corinthians 5:17–19; and Colossians 1:21–22 refer to making us acceptable to God. These passages describe our transition from being enemies to being friends. We were enemies of God due to our sin. Through forgiveness by the blood of Christ we were brought back to oneness with God. We are now no longer enemies, but friends.

This Scripture is the encompassing truth for us as Christians. We are restored sinners. True reconciliation with God as to our infertility comes as we accept His will for our lives, with or without children. With this healing, we begin to plead with Him, not about what we want, but about what *He* wants. Herein lies peace. We have found this stage of grief to be tremendously refreshing. We have come to the realization that God's will for our lives is not only preferable to anything we might want for ourselves but is also the very best plan. Reconciliation is complete freedom from struggling with the "Why's?" We may not understand "why" until we reach heaven, but we find at this stage that the "why" is not as important as simply resting and relaxing in God's will. We pray that you also may release your brokenness to Him at this stage and experience true rest and consoling.

Praise God! *We don't have to be controlled by our sorrow, but our sorrow can be used for the good of ourselves, others, and the kingdom of God!* If you have picked up this book, we have to believe that you have a desire to move beyond where you are emotionally and spiritually. Don't settle for stagnation. Don't settle for not bearing fruit. If you are a Christian, God, the vinedresser, is pruning you. He is fertilizing and preparing you. He has not called you to be stagnant but has equipped you to be a fruit-bearer. We rejoice with you as you experience growth and the fruits of life from your pruning.

Application Questions

1. *How have you allowed God to use your struggle with infertility to better minister to others? Give several examples.*

2. *How do you feel about integrating your infertility grief into your faith? Journal your thoughts and feelings.*

3. *What fruit do you already see being produced as a result of integrating your infertility grief into your faith?*

If you are producing no fruit, what is hindering you? What will you do about that hindrance starting today?

4. *Think of a time when God used you as a vessel to encourage or minister to someone else. How did this make you feel? How did this impact your relationship with your heavenly Father? What impact did this experience have on your grief?*

5. *What motherly characteristics has God gifted you with that He may be desiring to use to reach others? In what ways will you allow Him to use them for His purposes?*

Victory Verses

"Each tree is recognized by its own fruit."
—LUKE 6:44

"Thus, by their fruit you will recognize them."
—MATTHEW 7:20

Take heed to the ministry which thou hast received in the Lord, that thou fulfil it.
—COLOSSIANS 4:17 KJV

My brothers and sisters, whenever you face trials of any kind, consider it nothing but joy, because you know that the testing of your faith produces endurance; and let endurance have its full effect, so that you may be mature and complete, lacking in nothing.
—JAMES 1:2–4 NRSV

He called the crowd with His disciples, and said to them, "If any want to become my followers, let them deny themselves and take up their cross and follow me."
—MARK 8:34 NRSV

FROM HOPE TO ACTION

Pray for specific opportunities to minister to others, integrating your grief into your faith testimony. Pray for opportunities to minister to your spouse, friends, and colleagues. When an opportunity comes along, go after it, and witness your own healing take place!

8

DOES TIME
HEAL ALL WOUNDS?

We've all heard the cliché "Time heals all wounds." Certainly, emotional wounds do take time to heal, but if time were *all* that was needed, people wouldn't suffer from emotional storms all their lives. We think it is more accurate to say, "Faith in action heals all wounds." You see, you can suffer inactively all your life, or you can put your trust in God into action to bring you through your storm of grief. Time alone does not heal; it is the *faith-based action within a time period* that heals.

In this chapter, we want to discuss specific actions that can serve as catalysts for your healing. We have placed these strategies into three categories. First are *physical* coping techniques. These strategies are hands-on tasks that will help you move toward freedom. These tasks are specific and measurable. Second are *emotional* coping strategies that encourage Christ-centered stability. Third are *spiritual* coping strategies. These strategies point those in grief toward the ultimate healer and Great Physician, Jesus Christ. The three strategies—physical, emotional, and spiritual—must work together and be in balance. However, spiritual coping strategies must be the foundation. Christ is the core of our healing. This spiritual focus is our only assurance of victorious living.

Though Satan would choose to imprison you in your wounds, God has given you a free will. This free will allows you to choose to wallow in your grief or to take action toward healing. The strategies in this chapter are attainable and realistic. We have intentionally begun with the least threatening strategies, the ones easiest to implement. As you read, will you choose to act, using these strategies, to move out of your grief? Be encouraged in knowing that beginning with just one strategy will have a domino effect. Your choice to act on one strategy will give you the incentive and energy to act on the other strategies. Taking the first step will cause a chain reaction that will result in emotional healing.

PHYSICAL FAITH-BASED ACTIONS

1. *Be physically active.* Physical exercise has a significant, positive impact on our emotional health. In fact, God has made us so that a natural antidepressant is released when we exercise our bodies. Choose the activity that suits you best. A brisk walk may help you clear your mind and release tension. Take your dog for a walk or get on the treadmill while you watch your favorite show. Join a water aerobics class at a local fitness center. Consider an exercise group that will hold you accountable to your fitness goals.

Set realistic goals for your physical exercise. For example, start with ten to fifteen minutes at a time, three times a week. Make sure that you consult with your physician before beginning an exercise program. And be assured that your choice to exercise will lesson your pain and start the healing process.

2. *Eat nutritiously.* Grief is stressful and thus harmful to your physical health, so it is important that you do your part to take care of the vessel God has given you. Strive to eat a well-balanced diet with plenty of fruits

and vegetables. If maintaining balanced nutrition is a weakness for you, perhaps you could consult with a health educator or nutritionist for advice. Pray for God to direct you to the best program for your nutritional needs.

3. *Consider getting a pet.* Part of your desire to be a parent is the desire to nurture and be nurtured. Pets are certainly no substitute for your loss, but they are great companions and give unconditional acceptance.

4. *Keep a growth journal.* Journaling is a nonthreatening method of venting. Refer to some of the journal entries included in this book as examples of this type of journaling. Write out your innermost emotions and prayers to God, and watch how He heals you over time. Notice how your focus changes from being self-centered to Christ-centered. If writing is not your forte, make sure you are speaking your emotions and prayers aloud in your time alone with God. However, we recommend also writing these out, both for your recollection and to track your progress.

5. *Plan for expected times of grieving.* Have special, committed time with your spouse at the end of each menstrual cycle. Plan a trip for Mother's and Father's Day weekends both to grieve your loss and to celebrate your relationship with your spouse. Anticipate the grief of holidays and the anniversaries of miscarriages. Choose not to wallow in your wounds but focus on what you have to celebrate. Allow God to direct you through this emotional transition (Isaiah 61:1–3).

6. *Establish symbols for your grief.* Tangible symbols of your loss will help you gain resolution to your grief. For example, if you experience a miscarriage, have a memorial and burial, both tangible symbols of loss. Get creative with your spouse in inventing an intimate symbol for your infertility grief.

7. *Find your spiritual gift and join God where He is working.* You do not have to be a biological parent to have purpose in your life. Don't wait to be a mother before you allow yourself to be used by God. Don't be

WATER FROM THE ROCK

stagnant. Don't waste your talents and time waiting for children. Get active in what God is doing around you. If you stay inactive, you may miss God's best for your life. God's best involves your being active in His will and walking in obedience to Him. Ask your pastor for a spiritual gifts inventory that will help you discern where God has gifted you. Then, through prayer and consultation with your pastor, see where you can plug those gifts into your local church. Spend your time being useful to God rather than mourning what is absent from your life.

EMOTIONAL FAITH-BASED ACTIONS

1. *Expect confusion of feelings.* Your emotions will be confused and jumbled for, with infertility, the grief process doesn't have time to complete itself before it starts again with the next menstrual cycle. Some days you may feel angry. Other days you may cry at the drop of a hat. When your grief is the most intense, you may feel that you are losing your mind. You may experience insomnia, a change in appetite, or difficulty concentrating. At times you will feel bombarded by grief; at other times you will feel at peace. If you find that you are in a *constant* state of confusion, remember that "God is not a God of disorder but of peace" (1 Corinthians 14:33). You may be fighting a spiritual battle. *Trust your faith above your feelings* and fight the temptation to allow your jumbled emotions to guide you. Emotions and feelings are important, but they are not always based on truth.

2. *Allow yourself the right to grieve.* Grief will happen. If you deny it, it will wait for you. It will not go away. "Blessed are those who mourn, for they will be comforted" (Matthew 5:4). In His Word, God addresses the necessity of grieving and follows up with a promise to console. Jesus wept in His grief over the death of His friend Lazarus. Hannah, Elizabeth, and Sarah grieved immensely as they struggled with infertility. Why should we be any different?

We must realize that infertility is a loss and that it is normal to grieve losses. God created us with the capacity to feel difficult emotions. We must trust that He knew what He was doing when He gave us the capacity to mourn. We must realize also that even though we need to grieve over our losses, we need not be held captive by our grief. Our grief is to be with us for a time, but ultimately we are called to liberty (Isaiah 61:1). Be aware that once you gain freedom from your grief, it may re-occur. This return is normal. Be prepared for the possibility of the return of your grief, knowing that each time it will be easier to turn your burdens over to God.

3. *Don't put off coping.* Putting off coping with your grief will prevent you from experiencing the joy of your salvation. As a Christian, you are a child of God. You deserve to cope, and God is waiting to give you whatever you need to heal. Your freedom is just one choice away. This book is filled with suggestions that you can use to help you cope at a healthier level. However, you will not begin to cope with your grief until you *choose* to cope with your grief. Once you've made this decision, be intentional about implementing strategies that will help you move forward.

4. *Don't confuse your feelings with the facts of God's truth.* Your feelings may leave you grieved and sorrowful, filled with a sense of hopelessness, inadequacy, and worthlessness. Don't confuse those emotions with the fact that God created you and loves you beyond what you can comprehend. Jesus also suffered beyond what you can comprehend, because of His love for you. He *will* be faithful. Make sure that you are immersed in the Word. Unless you maintain a regular time of study, you will not have the truth in your mind. Don't allow yourself to be brainwashed by Satan's lies or your emotions but be washed in the truth of God's love. Quote scriptural truths; this is an effective offensive strategy against the schemes of Satan (Ephesians 6:17–18; 2 Timothy 1:7). Celebrate because Satan's fleeing frees you for healing.

5. *Reach out to others.* If you are focused on the needs of others, you cannot be self-absorbed in your own grief. With God's guidance, reach out to others who are hurting or who have various needs in their lives. God will lead you to someone you can help. Perhaps there is a colleague

who is struggling, or a neighbor, a relative, an acquaintance, or even a perfect stranger. You don't have to look far to see pain in the world. Find out what is going on in their lives and pray with them about the pain they are experiencing. Not only will this be a wonderful gift to them, but empathizing with someone else's pain will give perspective to your own.

6. *Get professional help if necessary.* Seek a qualified Christian counselor for support in marital strain, self-esteem issues, and spiritual struggles. Ask your pastor or physician for a referral if necessary. If you are seeing a fertility specialist, he or she may be able to refer you to a Christian counselor who specializes in infertility grief. Do not equate seeking help with weakness, but see it as a sign of courage. It takes a lot of strength to get help when you need it. Getting professional help may be a huge step in your healing.

Spiritual Faith-Based Actions

1. *Express your feelings of confusion or anger to God.* Put your questions at the foot of the cross. God can handle it! Expect this crisis to challenge your faith, but don't allow it to weaken your faith. Give Christ your heart and life and ask Him to help you reach a level of reconciliation. As you express yourself to God, remember what He has already told you in His Word: "The LORD is close to the brokenhearted and saves those who are crushed in spirit" (Psalm 34:18). "Cast all your anxiety on him because he cares for you" (1 Peter 5:7). "Don't be afraid; just believe" (Mark 5:36). Cling to Christ, who created you fully acceptable to Him with a unique purpose in life. Ask God to show you your true significance and believe what He tells you about who He created you to be.

2. *Establish a Christian support system.* Unite with others who have experienced similar grief. Join a Bible study group or a support group. Use the material provided in *Water from the Rock* as a springboard for discussion. Establish a relationship with at least one person who can relate to your struggle. Express to that person your feelings of loss, and sup-

port her in her loss. Gain objective, godly feedback regarding your feelings and motivations for action.

3. *Believe, despite the fog.* Cling to God when you cannot see the path ahead and do not feel like clinging. You may not be able to see through the fog of your storm, but God can. You may be scared to walk through the fog alone, but you don't have to fear walking through the fog alongside your Savior. Just as the sunshine clears the fog, so Jesus, God's Son, clears our fears and lifts our burdens. The Scriptures remind us, "Your word is a lamp to my feet and a light for my path" (Psalm 119:105). So part of clinging to God is being daily immersed in His Word. Hebrews 4:12 teaches us the power of God's Word: "For the word of God is living and active. Sharper than any double-edged sword." God's Word shows us His vision for our lives, and our faith is strengthened as we depend on His vision instead of our own.

Trust God's character. "We know that God causes all things to work together for good to those who love God, to those who are called according to His purpose" (Romans 8:28 NASB). "'For I know the plans I have for you,' declares the Lord, 'plans to prosper you and not to harm you, plans to give you hope and a future'" (Jeremiah 29:11). God will bring growth from your grief. Consciously look for the growth and trust Him.

4. *Soak yourself in the Word.* Learn about God's compassion and love for you as His child. Seek to learn more about God's character and how He responds to the trials and sorrows of His children. Learn about Jesus' experiences with grief and His instructions for how to cope. You will discover that as you soak in the Word, your wounds will heal for you will be saturated with His love.

5. *Realize that your situation does not have to change in order for you to proceed to the next level of the grief process.* Do not wait for your circumstance to improve before you improve. God may not bless you with a pregnancy, but you still can move beyond your grief into growth. Growth is not dependent on your circumstances; it is dependent on your relationship with your Creator and your willingness to trust Him in your grief process.

6. *Don't waste your suffering.* Your trial will produce strength and endurance in you if you take advantage of the learning and lessons available. What a shame that it would be to waste the pain you have experienced. So allow God to use your trial to stimulate spiritual growth in yourself. Allow Him also to use your trial to reach others. If you are a Christian, others are watching you face your trial. You have the opportunity to witness to them, giving them strength and insight, which builds their faith. As you live out your faith in front of others, your example will allow them to endure their own trials, whatever they might be.

7. *Know that you can experience joy.* Realize that you *can* experience joy through the opportunity to suffer alongside Christ. Look at blessings around you, rather than at your crisis. You can experience joy in your circumstance. Write down the blessings that have come as a direct result of your crisis of infertility. Allow yourself to laugh: "A cheerful heart is good medicine, but a crushed spirit dries up the bones" (Proverbs 17:22). Don't place your identity in what you *don't* have. Place it in what you *do* have. Your identity should not be in your infertility but in Christ. This identity transformation will result in joy and freedom in whatever storm you face!

Application Questions

1. *Look at the list of* physical *strategies. What are you already doing to act on your grief? Which strategies seem out of reach for you?*
    Look at the list of emotional *strategies. What are you already doing to act on your grief? Which strategies seem out of reach for you?*
    Look at the list of spiritual *strategies. What are you already doing to act on your grief? Which strategies seem out of reach for you?*

2. *Have you put off coping? Have you put off acting on your grief? Why or why not?*

3. *Number five under Spiritual Strategies states that your situation does not have to change in order for you to move to the next stage of grief. Do you believe this? Have you been waiting for your situation to change in order to have growth?*

4. *Who in your world can assist and support you as you begin putting action to your grief? How can you involve them in your healing?*

Victory Verse

"Come to me, all you who are weary and burdened, and I will give you rest."
—MATTHEW 11:28

FROM HOPE TO ACTION

Your action assignment is to pick one strategy from the lists in this chapter to begin doing this week. Commit yourself to this action, remembering that "faith in action heals wounds."

THE R'S OF
HEALING

9

RELATIONSHIP,
RECONCILIATION,
AND RESTORATION

In the previous chapters, we discussed the *grief process* of infertility. As our grief progresses, we are likely to experience damage to our significant relationships, our sense of self, our relationship with the heavenly Father, and even to our thought processes. This chaper and the following two chapters will focus on *healing* in those areas of our lives. As you proceed through this material, prayerfully consider your willingness to seek healing and your readiness for healing. Mark the strategies that might be most effective in your own personal healing. God bless you in your journey.

GOD DESIRES UNITY

If you are open to what God wants to reveal to you, you may learn that some of your relationships have suffered during your time of grief. You may have experienced relationship strains—a strained marriage, a strained relationship with family members, a tense relationship with friends. This strain and tension may have broken the bond of unity you once shared.

This lack of unity is not God's desire. We are reminded in Jesus' words to the disciples in the Upper Room of God's desire for unity: "I ask not only on behalf of these, but also on behalf of those who will believe in me through their word, *that they may all be one*. As you, Father, are in me and I am in you, may they also be in us, so that the world may believe that you have sent me" (John 17:20–21 NRSV, italics added). God further demonstrates for us the importance and power of unity in His own oneness with Jesus and the Holy Spirit.

We are reminded in the Sermon on the Mount of the everlasting significance of our decision to reconcile relationships: "You have heard that it was said, 'Love your neighbor and hate your enemy.' But I tell you: Love your enemies and pray for those who persecute you, that you may be sons of your Father in heaven" (Matthew 5:43–45). We must keep an eternal perspective as we consider the hurts and bruises in our relationships.

This restoration of relationships is only one part of the healing process. In this chapter we will discuss seven strategies for relationship reconciliation and also the importance of forgiveness and taking the lead in seeking reconciliation.

All of the strategies are easy to remember because each starts with the letter *R*. They are physical approaches. All are verbs. Verbs denote action taken by the subject. As you review these godly strategies, consider the relationships in your life that need to be nurtured. Open your heart to be one of willingness and surrender to the lordship of Jesus Christ regarding these strategies in your wounded relationships.

THE R'S OF REPAIRING
WOUNDED RELATIONSHIPS

1. *Reveal* the relationships that need reconciliation. This revelation can only come with the help of the Holy Spirit. Therefore, reconcilia-

tion must start with prayer. Ask God to show you which relationships in your life are characterized by division. This awareness of problems is the foundation for restoration.

Once you have determined which relationships have division in them, ask the Holy Spirit to release His wisdom in order for you to make a godly decision regarding reconciliation. James 1:5 tells us, "If any of you is lacking in wisdom, ask God, who gives to all generously and ungrudgingly, and it will be given you" (NRSV). Search the facts about the relationship and pray over what you find. Is this relationship "unequally yoked" (2 Corinthians 6:14 KJV)? Are you both believers? If this relationship were reconciled, would it push you closer to Christ or pull you further away? Before your division, was Christ the center of the relationship? If not, what *was* the center of the relationship? The divisions in your relationships may be a result of your own sin or the sin of someone else. The divisions may be a result of others avoiding your grief and, therefore, separating themselves from you.

Regardless of the source, a division, slight or otherwise, may have occurred and needs attention. You may realize that a close friend from church now avoids eye contact with you. Or maybe your relationship with a relative has a more formal tone than before. Perhaps you notice more irritability and conflict in your marriage than before. Ask God to sharpen your sensitivity to what is happening in the relationships in your life.

2. *Realize* any wrongdoing on your part. Search yourself for any sin in your life that may have created the division in the relationship (Psalm 139:23–24). Remember, it is not always your sin that leads to division, but it is certainly a possible cause of the separation and therefore deserves consideration. In the process of infertility grief, it is common to be so self-focused that you are vulnerable to sin. Out of jealousy toward others, you may have ignored them. You may have left them out, or turned a cold shoulder toward them. You may have isolated yourself in your grief and made yourself unavailable to those with whom you once had a close relationship. You may have avoided family out of embarrassment at being unable to produce a new generation. You may have categorized others

and yourselves according to your fertility. You may have forced people, including yourself, into cliques.

In your marriage relationship, you may have placed the blame for your infertility on your partner. As a result of this blame, you may have treated your spouse disrespectfully, as "second-class." Perhaps you have taken a friend for granted or used your relationship with that friend for the wrong purposes. Perhaps you have hurt someone without even realizing it. Remember, you have a responsibility not to be a stumbling block to your brother or sister in Christ (Romans 14:21). Sin comes in many disguises, so take some time to really search yourself and your broken relationships. If you can identify that you have sinned against someone, ask God to forgive you and then move on to the next *R*.

3. *Record* your trials and triumphs in previous relationships to assist you in improving your present relationships. Look back on past relationships that were reconciled. Think about previous relationships with family and friends. Think about times when you overcame obstacles in your marriage. Who was involved in the reconciliation? What caused the division? How did restoration take place? What steps did you take to reunite?

Use this information to brainstorm ideas for reconciling your current relationship. Make notes about your ideas. Think about the root of the division. Consider the personality, background, and temperament of the other party. How approachable is he or she? How can you express yourself to that person in a way that will be understood and the other person can receive and appreciate? Ask God to help you develop ideas that will reach this person and prevent further division.

Write out your ideas and then narrow your choices. Cross out the ideas that, after further prayer, you see will not assist in reconciliation. Pray about the best approach for this particular relationship division. Make a choice and a commitment to act on that approach.

Then, as Scripture requires, go to the person with whom there is a breach. If this person is your brother or sister in Christ, then seek reconciliation as a member of the "family." If this person is not a Christian, this initiation gives you the opportunity to be a witness for Christ and may teach the other person how much God desires reconciliation. Remember: reconciliation is not an option; it is a ministry, and you are called as an ambassador of God to be reconciled with others. "He has committed to us the message of reconciliation. We are therefore Christ's ambassadors, as though God were making his appeal through us" (2 Corinthians 5:19–20).

4. *Refuse* to act in a negative manner. If you were able to identify your own sin as being the root of the division, ask your friend, family member, or spouse to forgive you. Refuse to continue the sin in your life that you identified in step 2. Refuse to act in a way that would negate your attempts to reconcile. Refuse to gossip. Refuse to murmur. Refuse to hold a grudge. Give your jealousy and envy to God, and ask for a grateful, satisfied heart.

It is easier to become stuck and stagnant than it is to grow. You must go against the grain of your sinful nature. If you don't, you risk making a bad situation worse and becoming bitter. We are instructed in God's Word, "Looking diligently lest . . . any root of bitterness springing up trouble you, and thereby many be defiled" (Hebrews 12:15 KJV). A root can do two things: it can provide nourishment and strength or it can strangle and stunt growth. The "root of bitterness" strangles relationship life and leads to death. Refuse to be consumed by the "root" of bitterness. Refuse to focus on division, and allow God to refocus your heart, mind, and energy toward reunification.

Expect a struggle within yourself. Satan wants to continue your division, and he will attack your efforts to change your focus. Satan would love to see your struggle with infertility create a permanent separation between you and others. He is at war to accomplish that. In the name of Jesus, refuse to give Satan the victory.

5. *Release* God's love to the unlovely. The only way to release God's love to others is if you are walking with Him. Allow God's Holy Spirit to be "increased" within you so that He can be "released" through you. Once you are filled with His presence and His precious Holy Spirit, then you can allow yourself to be a spilled-out vessel to pour God's love upon others.

Don't be selfish with God's love; there is plenty to share. The beauty of Jesus in you can be what draws and attracts people to you. If the other party in your wounded relationship does not respond to your attempts to love him, keep loving him anyway (Matthew 5:43–48). Pray for him. Know that in your obedience you are planting a seed of transformation. The effect of this obedience and unconditional spilling out of God's love is personal healing. Releasing God's love to others will help you work through your own personal grief regarding your infertility.

6. *Raise* your focus. Look to Christ and let His thoughts be your thoughts (Isaiah 55:8–9). Pray for His desires to become your desires. Raise yourself out of your own fleshly circumstances and into a heavenly perspective (Psalm 121). Keep your eyes on the Problem-solver, not your problem. Helen Lemmel wrote these words in the chorus of her inspirational hymn:

> Turn your eyes upon Jesus,
> Look full in His wonderful face;
> And the things of earth will grow strangely dim
> In the light of His glory and grace.

Oh, how the situation looks different when your *eyes are on the Savior!* Oh, how the situation looks different when you begin to *see it through Christ's eyes.* Oh, how the situation looks different when you've *given your burdens to God!*

In 1 Peter 5:7, God asks you to cast "all your care upon him; for he careth for you" (KJV). Rise up with the help of the Holy Spirit. Consider the needs of the other person in the wounded relationship. What are his or her trials? Hurts? Struggles? Be prepared to provide the other person with comfort as he or she grieves personal losses. The person may be experiencing overwhelming emotions regarding his or her role as a parent. Or perhaps the person is facing a serious physical illness or contemplating a career change. In other words, there are people around you every day facing their own set of griefs.

Second Corinthians 1:3–4 shows us that grief is actually an opportunity to comfort others and encourage unity. "Blessed be the God and Father of our Lord Jesus Christ, the Father of mercies and the God of all consolation, who consoles us in all our affliction, so that we may be able to console those who are in any affliction with the consolation with which we ourselves are consoled by God" (NRSV). Your infertility grief may have created some division, but the division does not have to continue. Prepare yourself to serve. Again, you will find this strategy to be helpful in your own healing of grief. It is a very powerful transformation when you lay down your own struggles, notice the trials of those surrounding you, and take on the role of service.

7. *Reach out* and put action to your desires for reconciliation. God fulfilled the ultimate "reaching out" when He restored the broken relationship with mankind. "All this is from God, who reconciled us to himself through Christ and gave us the ministry of reconciliation" (2 Corinthians 5:18). God identified the problem of sin and gave His Son as the solution. In the same way, you are called to identify the problems in your relationships and be obedient in acting on the solutions God shows to you. This calling is the ministry of reconciliation.

There is nothing technical about reaching out. The key is persistence. Persistence proves your seriousness. Be diligent in your reaching out; your efforts may not work in your first attempt. Communicate with one another about your relationship struggle. Have open and honest conversation about the tension or strain in the relationship. Devote time and energy to the relationship. Invest in the relationship as you would a prized possession, because that is exactly what it is.

Acknowledge the importance of the presence of that precious someone in your life. Reach out to a friend with a phone call or an invitation to lunch. Reach out to a spouse with a personal letter or a back rub. Reach out to a family member with a compliment or a word of encouragement. Be real and genuine, and be obedient to do whatever God tells you to do.

YOU MUST TAKE THE LEAD

In order to overcome injured relationships with others, you must take the lead in restoring unity. This initiation of a restoration will not only open the door to healing and forgiveness but will also allow you to move beyond the emotional hurts that have caused you pain.

Jesus says in the Lord's Prayer that we must forgive those who have trespassed against us, and He reminds us to ask Him to forgive us of our own wrongdoing. Therefore, as Christians, resolving broken relationships with others is essential to our relational oneness with God. How can we have a clean slate with God if we hold a grudge against a brother or a sister? Matthew 5:23–24 teaches that we must attempt reconciliation with our brother or sister in Christ before offering our sacrifices to God. Then we can truly worship Christ with a pure heart.

Perhaps you do not feel like restoring a particular relationship. Do not wait until you *feel* like it to make this choice. Why don't *you* be the initiator of the mending process? In the following acronym, Y–O–U are the one to begin the restoration.

> **Y**ield to God
> **O**vercome your broken relationship
> **U**nite with God and others

You be the one to initiate peace and restoration through your obedience. This yielding will allow God to use you to bring *beauty* out of the *ashes* of your broken relationships (Isaiah 61:3).

Having attempted reconciliation in a broken relationship, you may or may not see results. But God is still working, no matter what results you see. If you see positive results in the relationship, rejoice with the other person and give God the glory for the healing. If you don't see positive results, rejoice still because you have been obedient and have planted a seed. If you do not receive positive results, you cannot be responsible for the rejection of your attempt. You can only be responsible for initiating and persisting in your attempts. Once you have obeyed God in reaching out for the healing of the relationship, you can rest in the peace of God. You have carried out your responsibility. It is now the choice of the other party to respond to your obedience.

BE FORGIVING

Not only do we have the task of taking the lead in initiating restoration, we also have a mandate and a responsibility to offer forgiveness to others for all hurts. If someone comes to you requesting forgiveness for a sin that has caused a division between the two of you, you are called to forgive that person. This action is not an option but a must for Christians, since our very faith is based on Christ's forgiveness of us.

In Matthew 18:23–35, Jesus tells the story of a man who had many debts. The king chose to forgive him of a great amount of his debt. In the next instant, this very man was approached by someone who owed him a small amount and asked to have the debt forgiven—and he refused. In his pride, the man who had many debts did not extend to someone else the forgiveness he himself had just received. In the same way, how can we, who have been forgiven so much, be so proud as not to forgive others? This receiving and offering of forgiveness is the basis of reconciling and restoring relationships.

You may sometimes be rejected in your attempts to reconcile an earthly relationship that has been divided by infertility. However, you will never experience rejection in your attempts to reconcile your relationship with your heavenly Father through Jesus Christ. Even if your friends or family have no interest in reconciling, even if your spouse has no interest in reconciling, *God* is eagerly awaiting your response. He is always anticipating, with open arms, your reconciliation with Him.

Application Questions

1. *Make a list of any relationships in your life in which there is friction. Determine the cause of this friction.*
   How has this friction affected your relationship with God?
   What are some steps that you could take to eliminate friction in these particular relationships?

2. *As discussed in this chapter, forgiveness is the foundation of relationships. Whom do you need to forgive? Are you willing to accept their offer of forgiveness?*
   Do you need to ask someone to forgive you?

3. *Have you ever initiated reconciliation and been rejected?*
   How did you handle that?
   Were you pleased with your reaction? Why or why not?

Victory Verses

Therefore if thou bring thy gift to the altar, and there remem-
berest that thy brother hath ought against thee; leave there
thy gift before the altar, and go thy way; first be reconciled to
thy brother, and then come and offer thy gift.
—MATTHEW 5:23–24 KJV

FROM HOPE TO ACTION

Your action assignment is to apply the R's
in this chapter to your healing. Make a
choice to heed the Holy Spirit in His leading
you to initiate reconciliation with one of
the relationships listed in question number
one in the Application Questions section in
this chapter. Keep in mind that this step of
reconciliation is crucial to your personal
healing, your relationship with your spouse,
your relationship with your forgiving Savior,
and your personal spiritual growth.

10

RENEWING
YOUR MIND

If you have experienced a crisis of infertility, then it is likely you
have also experienced periods of emotional defeat as your
thoughts have become your enemy. Often in our trial of childlessness, we struggle with self-defeating thoughts, debilitating
comparisons, and depressing untruths. If you are to gain freedom
in your storm of infertility, you must first experience a renewal
of your mind.

As you begin this chapter, we invite you to turn with us to
Acts 16:25–34. Paul and Silas are in Philippi and have been
brought before the civil magistrates after casting out a demon
in the name of Jesus. The authorities have stripped and flogged
them and put them into jail with their feet in stocks. Despite
this experience, we see them at midnight, "praying and singing
hymns to God" (v. 25). They worshiped even in a difficult time,
finding God to be worthy of their praise. They trusted in the

perfect, acceptable will of God. They knew the Most High God, took on the mind of Christ, and relied on the guidance of the Holy Spirit. Their focus allowed them to understand that, despite their circumstances, God was in control and His work was not complete.

Imagine the impact their response to their situation had on the prisoners who witnessed this service of praise. Even when the doors of the prison were opened and they had the chance to be released, they did not walk away! They realized that running from the difficulty was not the best way out. Their actions as Christians caused the jailer to take notice. He began to desire for himself what he saw in them. As a result, the jailer and his entire family were brought to salvation (v. 34).

How do you explain the attitude of Paul and Silas in the midst of torture? Their attitude was the result of a renewed mind. Their renewed minds caused them to focus on the eternal instead of their immediate surroundings. But how did they achieve this renewal? Romans 12:2 says, "Do not conform any longer to the pattern of this world, but be transformed by the renewing of your mind." The word *transformed* implies that this renewal is a *process* rather than an event. The purpose of this chapter is to review this process of renewal. We challenge you to examine your own thought patterns as we proceed. Do you have the "mind of Christ" (1 Corinthians 2:16 KJV)? Are your thoughts transformed and renewed? If not, how is this mind-set affecting your daily walk through your grief? As in the previous chapter, we will review this process using seven easy-to-remember verbs starting with the letter *R*.

THE R'S OF RENEWAL

1. *Resist* Satan's lies and reject the patterns of this world. Perhaps the most difficult aspect of infertility is the struggle within the mind. Naturally, we try to find answers and place blame for what seems to be an unfair trial. This response is dangerous and destructive. Satan rules worldly patterns, and God warns us not to conform to those patterns (Romans 12:2). Why is this nonconforming important? Because Satan desires to defeat and destroy us in our grief. He will cause us to compare ourselves to others and lead us to feel insignificant and inadequate when

we don't think we measure up to someone else. He will cause us to blame ourselves for our childlessness. He will attempt to divide our marriage relationships and our friendships. If we are to thrive in our grief, we must resist the tendency to believe Satan, who is nothing but a liar.

How do we resist and reject him? Read the Word. Read the Word. And read the Word some more. We *must* be saturated with the truth in order to discern and reject the lie. We must claim the truth and speak it out loud when we are feeling defeated. When we are weak, we need to remember this verse: "For God hath not given us the spirit of fear; but of power, and of love, and of a sound mind" (2 Timothy 1:7 KJV).

2. *Rest* in the comfort of the Holy Spirit. Fighting the thoughts that defeat you is an exhausting experience. In fact, it is an experience you absolutely cannot conquer on your own. Don't forget—God sent a comforter. When you are weary, go to Him. When your burden is more than you can carry, give it to Him. When you feel as though you are losing your mind, ask the Holy Spirit to cleanse your thoughts and give you peace. You are not alone. He is always present and available. When you are not sure if the thoughts you are having are truthful or not, pray for discernment. Remember, when Jesus told His disciples about the Holy Spirit, He referred to Him as "the Spirit of truth" (John 14:17). Therefore, the Holy Spirit is not only a source of comfort and consoling but also a source of truth when truth is difficult to discern.

3. *Resolve* inner conflicts, releasing regrets and unforgiveness and repenting of self-focus. Perhaps there are old personal issues that have never been resolved. Previous hurts, disappointments, and betrayals can creep up with great intensity when you are in the midst of a trial. Make a commitment to work through these issues, whatever it takes, so that they do not further complicate your infertility grief. If this task takes professional assistance, that is OK.

Perhaps you have regrets about previous sins in your life, or maybe you hold a grudge against someone for a sin committed against you. How is it helping you to continue to hold on to this baggage? It is probably not helping at all. In fact, it is probably a significant hindrance to your healing. Commit to releasing yourself and others through forgiveness. Go to God with a heart of repentance because you have allowed these conflicts to interfere with your relationship with Him. With a pure heart, you can be freed to heal, and your relationship with your Savior will blossom.

4. *Reframe* your situation from a spiritual perspective. The struggle within our minds occurs because we depend upon our limited understanding to explain complex life situations. If we are to gain victory in our thoughts, we must depend on the perspective of the One who has infinite understanding rather than depending on the limitations of our human minds.

From a human perspective there is no logical explanation for the fact that some irresponsible individuals can easily become pregnant while God-fearing, established couples are unable to conceive. Yet, we must resist the temptation to depend on logic. God's understanding has no limits (Psalm 147:5). So we must pray to see our confusing situation from His eternal perspective. "Trust in the LORD with all your heart and lean not on your own understanding," Proverbs 3:5 commands us.

It is not wise to depend on what we can see and how we can make sense of our situation. The Lord declares in Isaiah 55:8, "My thoughts are not your thoughts, neither are your ways my ways." So we must, through faith, reframe our situation through the mind of Christ. We must look beyond the obvious into a bigger, eternal perspective.

5. *Restore* godly thinking and renew your attitude. Now that you have resisted Satan's attacks and reframed your trial of infertility, you can begin to focus your thoughts in a more godly manner. We believe this godly thinking is what Paul was referring to when he told his brothers in Christ, "Finally, brothers, whatever is true, whatever is noble, whatever is right, whatever is pure, whatever is lovely, whatever is admirable—if anything is excellent or praiseworthy—think about such things" (Philippians 4:8).

Paul understood the importance and influence of our thoughts. We challenge you with the same instruction. Measure your thoughts with this verse of Scripture. Ask yourself, "In regard to my infertility, are my thoughts true . . . noble . . . right . . . pure . . . lovely . . . admirable . . .

excellent . . . praiseworthy?" If not, pray immediately that God would restore your thoughts and renew your attitude.

6. *Rely* on others. This step is important, but it has to be carefully implemented or it will do more harm than good. It is important to have others around you who can hold you accountable to truthful thoughts—but not just anyone is qualified for this task.

First, this person must be someone in which you can confide, someone you can trust to keep your intimate thoughts to herself.

Second, this person must be spiritually mature. How can someone who is not thoroughly familiar with the truth possibly help you to discern truth? This individual must be someone who is guided by the Holy Spirit and in a growing relationship with the Lord Jesus Christ.

Third, this person must be someone who has a positive effect on you. In other words, this person must be capable of holding you accountable for your thoughts in a way you feel comfortable receiving and to which you can respond to peacefully. When you spend time with this person you should be encouraged and energized rather than annoyed and hindered. If you do not have someone like this in your life right now, pray that God would provide this resource for you.

7. *Remember* the One to whom you should run for daily renewal. Though fellowship with an accountability partner is helpful, fellowship with God is essential. The process of transforming your mind requires daily renewal. Though you *cannot* become dependent on an accountability partner, you *must* become dependent on God if you want to experience true renewal. Run back to your heavenly Father when you are tempted to focus on the negative aspects of your trial. Run back, trusting that your Father can change your defeatist thinking patterns.

The amount of time it takes for your mind to become transformed is directly correlated to your willingness to submit to His teachings. The more time you spend in His Word and in communication with Him through prayer, the sooner you will succeed in this mental renewal. Be encouraged—this mental transformation is a process that will take you from trials to triumphs, from valleys to victories, from friction to freedom.

HELP FROM OUR HEAVENLY FATHER

In summary, our hope of overcoming stems from transforming our way of thinking about our trials. The renewing of our minds is in no way dependent on our circumstances being changed. A situation that has not changed at all can suddenly be improved as our way of thinking is renewed. For instance, we do not have to achieve pregnancy in order to experience a transformed mind. Just changing how we think about our infertility can cause us to experience it in a more positive manner. This transformation comes about when we make a daily choice to look for the "good" that is produced from our infertility. This choice can only occur as we are in living in line with God's will.

Think about the devastating trial Paul experienced as he was persecuted and imprisoned for declaring the gospel. Yet, he wrote to his brothers in Christ, "I have learned to be content whatever the circumstances. I know what it is to be in need, and I know what it is to have plenty. I have learned the secret of being content in any and every situation" (Philippians 4:11–12). Paul had a renewed mind and an eternal perspective—but only because he depended on God for his transformation. The result was a state of contentment and satisfaction. Though he was imprisoned, he was truly free in his storm.

Similarly, if we attempt to alter our thought patterns without the assistance of our heavenly Father, we may experience a temporary sense of relief but will quickly revert to our destructive ways of thinking. We will not experience the state of contentment Paul wrote about in the New Testament. We can only get so far in our own fleshly power. Our goal should be to become so thoroughly enmeshed with our heavenly Father that our way of thinking about our infertility matches His way of thinking. When we experience this transformed mind, we will also gain ground and experience true freedom in our storm of infertility.

Application Questions

1. Write out the thoughts you have about your infertility that are most destructive to you. Are these thoughts based on truth? What steps do you need to take to begin the process of renewing your thoughts?

2. Are there previous hurts from your past (self- or other-inflicted) that are hindering the renewal of your thoughts? What do you need to do to resolve the hurts caused by these burdens?

3. Pretend God was interviewed about your trial of infertility. What do you think He would have to say about it? How do you think His thoughts might differ from your own thoughts about your trial?

Victory Verses

"For my thoughts are not your thoughts,
neither are your ways my ways," declares the LORD.
—ISAIAH 55:8

Do not conform any longer to the pattern of this world,
but be transformed by the renewing of your mind.
Then you will be able to test and approve what
God's will is—his good, pleasing and perfect will.
—ROMANS 12:2

Sing and make music in your heart to the Lord,
always giving thanks to God the Father for everything,
in the name of our Lord Jesus Christ.
—EPHESIANS 5:19–20

I am not saying this because I am in need, for I have learned
to be content whatever the circumstances. I know what it is to
be in need, and I know what it is to have plenty. I have
learned the secret of being content in any and every situation.
—PHILIPPIANS 4:11–12

FROM HOPE TO ACTION

Write a letter as if it were being written
from God just to you. In the letter, focus on
how God might look at you and your trial
of infertility. Make sure the statements
in this letter are based on truth.
Keep your letter close at hand for times
when your mind is being attacked and
you need a reminder of the truth.

11

~

REFUGE
IN THE ROCK

When we think about the word *refuge,* feelings of safety and security come to mind. There is a sense of stability in the word. Refuge represents a peaceful haven to which we can flee. One would think that stability and infertility are mutually exclusive, yet they *can* coexist when Jesus is involved. You see, Jesus Christ is rock solid (1 Corinthians 10:3–4) and brings peace and stability to even the most devastating situations. "God is our refuge and strength, an ever-present help in times of trouble" (Psalm 46:1). "The LORD is a refuge for the oppressed, a stronghold in times of trouble" (Psalm 9:9).

Have you ever heard someone say that Satan had a stronghold in a particular struggle? On the basis of what 2 Corinthians 10:4–5 says, you probably have. Did you know that Jesus, your Savior, wants to be the stronghold in your struggle? Not only does He desire to be our strength, but Psalm 9:10 reminds us that our Lord can be trusted to be our refuge, for He will never forsake us.

As in the previous chapters, we will be leading you in this chapter to become fully grounded in Christ. Using seven easy-to-remember verbs, all starting with the letter *R,* let us begin our journey to ultimate security and stability through our infertility trial.

A Personal Relationship with Jesus Christ

First, however, we would like to speak with you regarding a personal relationship with Jesus Christ. Accepting Him as your personal Lord and Savior is the first step in trusting in Him as your refuge. If you have not already asked Him to come into your life and take it over, we would encourage you to do so now. Jesus came so that you would have new life and "have it more abundantly" (John 10:10 KJV). The God of the Universe sent His Son, Jesus, to die on a cross so that you could have eternal life. *God had to suffer the loss of a Child at that moment so that you could have all you need to claim victory in your life.*

Do you know the One who died on that cross? Do you have living in your heart the One who suffered deadly pain and ridicule? Do you realize that His shed blood can cleanse you from your sins? Jesus, the One who shed blood for you, went to hades and back so that you wouldn't have to suffer an eternity in hell. He made this sacrifice of Himself so that you could live an eternity in heaven with Him.

If you would like to know Jesus as your personal Lord and Savior, confess that to Him and ask Him to come into your life. The following prayer is a guide:

Dear Lord Jesus,

I am a sinner, and I know I cannot save myself. I believe that You died on a cross to save me from my sins and rose again on the third day. I ask You to forgive me of my sins, and take over my life. I love You, Jesus. Amen.

Having acknowledged that Jesus is the Son of the living God, you, like Peter, have the Rock upon which you can build (Matthew 16:16). Unlike the sand that shifts during the storms, this Rock is solid, complete, and eternal (Matthew 7:25–27).

So, now that you have access to the Rock that is Jesus Christ, how do you lean on Him to help you with your trial? Well, according to Matthew 7:24, you must put what you have learned into practice, resulting in wisdom. When you practice taking refuge in the Rock, no matter your storm, you will stand securely.

THE R'S OF REFUGE

Below are the seven R's that are your practical tools. Follow them as you take refuge in the rock of Christ through your storm.

1. *Read* God's Word daily. According to John 1:1, the Word is God; therefore, reading His Word allows you to know and understand Him at a deeper level. We must know the Rock before we can learn to trust Him. The Word of God is like no other book because no other book is "God-breathed" by the Holy Spirit (2 Timothy 3:16). The Word of God is powerful (Hebrews 4:12). Daily reading the Word of God will develop your faith (Romans 10:17).

If you do not already have a regular time for Bible study or a quiet time with God, meet with your pastor or a spiritually mature Christian friend to get you started. Just as getting to know your spouse and maintaining a relationship with him takes a daily commitment, so also maintaining your relationship with your Savior requires a daily commitment.

Find a translation of the Bible you can easily understand. A study Bible or a life-application Bible can be helpful. There are also thousands of suitable devotional guides available through your local Christian bookstore that can assist you in your study. Read Psalm 119 to understand the importance of the Word of God. Every verse in this psalm refers to the power of the Scriptures in providing guidance, comfort, and hope. Rest assured, your daily commitment to study will result in wisdom and maturity and leave you "equipped for every good work" (2 Timothy 3:14–17).

2. *Recognize* God's love for you. As you read God's Word, you will find that His love for you permeates the pages. Consider the following scriptural truths that demonstrate God's love for you.

According to John 3:16, God loved you so much "that he gave his one and only Son, that whoever believes in him shall not perish but have eternal life." The central focus of the gospel and of your salvation is God's loving sacrifice based on His love for you. Consider John 15:13, which says, "Greater love has no one than this, that he lay down his life for his friends." Romans 5:7–8 says, "Very rarely will anyone die for a righteous man, though for a good man someone might possibly dare to die. But God demonstrates his own love for us in this: While we were still sinners, Christ died for us." In other words, the ultimate act of love was demonstrated for us when Jesus shed His blood and died in order to cleanse us and forgive us of all our sin.

We are also comforted by Romans 8:38–39, which tells us, "I am convinced that neither death nor life, neither angels nor demons, neither the present nor the future, nor any powers, neither height nor depth, nor anything else in all creation, will be able to separate us from the love of God that is in Christ Jesus our Lord." Look at Matthew 10:29–31, which says, "Are not two sparrows sold for a penny? Yet not one of them will fall to the ground apart from the will of your Father. And even the very hairs of your head are all numbered. So don't be afraid; you are worth more than many sparrows."

Sometimes you may feel unloved. You may feel abandoned when you face a trial or are disciplined, but remember that God's discipline is always an act of love (Proverbs 3:11–12). Always refer to the truths of Scripture when you feel alone and unloved. You see, the Scriptures are proof of God's promise to love you. He has already done so much as a result of His love for you. God gave His Son . . . who came . . . and suffered . . . all out of love. As you recognize and understand God's love for you, you will feel more complete and gain perspective on your trial of infertility. Won't you run to the Rock? Won't you run to the One who loves you?

3. *Receive* the comfort and guidance of the Holy Spirit. The Holy Spirit was sent by God "to be with you forever" (John 14:16). Jesus described the Holy Spirit to His disciples in verse 17 of that same chapter as "the Spirit of truth." Earlier in the Gospel of John He also said that this Spirit "gives life" (John 6:63). The Holy Spirit is your "Counselor" (John 14:16) and assists you in discernment. He remains in you to teach you (1 John 2:20, 27). Not only that, but when you are feeling weak and don't even know how to pray, relax, for the Holy Spirit will be interceding for you (Romans 8:26–27).

Is the Holy Spirit available to you? According to the Scriptures, if you have accepted Christ, then you also have received the "gift of the Holy Spirit" (Acts 2:38). In Ephesians 1:13–14, you are reminded that the Holy Spirit will seal you until the day of redemption. You have been purchased, you have inherited the Holy Spirit, and you can *know* that you are His. Rely on this comfort and assurance as you courageously face your loss and the disappointment of childlessness.

4. *Reflect* on the blood of Christ. When is the last time you really thought in detail about the suffering our Savior experienced on His journey to Calvary and the crucifixion that followed? If you are like us, you often will take for granted the incredible sacrifice and the tremendous suffering our Savior experienced out of His love for you and me. We invite you to peruse Psalm 22:1–18. This psalm, quoted in the New Testament, prophesies the horrible suffering Christ endured. Can you imagine your hands and feet being pierced so that your body could hang from those nails until you suffocated? Can you imagine your bones being out of joint? Can you imagine your strength being wasted away? Can you imagine being so thirsty that your tongue sticks to the roof of your mouth? Can you imagine witnessing your clothing being divided as you look down upon your enemies and take your final breath? Can you imagine your love for someone being so misunderstood that he kills you?

All of this suffering happened to our Lord Jesus Christ. His red blood was spilled to make us "white as snow" (Isaiah 1:18)—so that our sins could be washed away. Most amazing to us is that Jesus *chose* to die this incredibly cruel death. He *chose* to leave a life of glory to walk this earth as a man. That was His plan. That was His will.

Why, then, is reflection on this gruesome event important? It is important because we need to realize that Christ *truly* knows and understands physical and emotional pain. He understands our struggles, because He faced the most horrible of struggles (Hebrews 2:18). He sympathizes with our pain, because He is familiar with living with pain (Isaiah 53:3; also Hebrews 4:15). Who better to lean on during your trial of infertility than the One who has experienced the ultimate trial of pain and suffering, for your sake, all without sin? As you ponder the sufferings Christ endured for you, you will come to realize just how valuable you are to Him. You are valuable just as you are.

5. *Restore* the joy of your salvation. Yes, you were lovingly purchased by the blood of Christ, so rejoice in your precious gift of salvation! If you have received Him, you *are* His child. God gave up His own Son so that you could become His. What a comforting thought! The Holy Spirit testifies to the fact that you are a child of God (Romans 8:16). This acceptance as His child means that you do not have to submit to fear but can safely and assuredly nestle in the arms of your "*Abba,* Father" (v. 15). Your life on this earth is a fleeting, temporary mission that you live as you look forward to the reward of your salvation—a life of eternity in the presence of your heavenly Father. Don't allow the disappointments of this temporary life to rob you of the joy of the life eternal to which you look forward.

6. *Refine* your character. According to the dictionary, character is a quality or trait that distinguishes an individual. What qualities or traits currently define who you are? Are you fully pleased with your list of qualities? If not, your trial is an opportunity for these traits to be refined. In Isaiah 48:10, the Lord reminds the people of Israel that it is through the "furnace of affliction" that they are "refined." It is through the heat of our trials that we are purified and our character is tested, strengthened, and established.

Perhaps you sometimes feel that God is "turning up the furnace." Rest assured, as you face your trial with faith, God will peel away areas of weakness as He molds you into the image of His Son. Remember, your refining takes place as you, the "clay," are molded by your Creator, the "potter" (Isaiah 64:8). You must continue to trust Him during your time in the furnace. The result will be a refreshing boldness, a renewed and strengthened faith, the fear of God, and the reputation of godly character. All of these qualities will prepare you for the final *R*.

7. *Rejoice* in the suffering. Yes, rejoice. This statement sounds like an oxymoron, but don't throw the book away. It *is* possible, even biblical, to rejoice in the midst of your sufferings. How? It starts with faith, which leads to an eternal focus (Romans 5:1–5). This focus permits you to praise and rejoice throughout your pain. We like to think of this focus as vertical, one centered on Christ and the promises to come. This focus is the opposite of a horizontal focus, one strictly centered on self and the surrounding circumstances. There is no doubt in my mind that our Savior had an eternal, vertical focus as He faced His trial of death. He endured "for the joy set before Him." He knew the end result of salvation made available to all, and He knew He'd soon be back in His home of glory in the presence of His Father.

What is most exciting to us is that we are called "co-heirs" ("joint heirs" KJV) if we are His children. Romans 8:16–17 proclaims, "The Spirit himself testifies with our spirit that we are God's children. Now if we are children, then we are heirs—heirs of God and co-heirs with Christ, if indeed we share in his sufferings in order that we may also share in his glory." Yes, we can rejoice because we are given the privilege of suffering alongside Christ that we might have eternal glory. This truth is incredibly comforting, but it takes faith to grasp it.

But there are still other reasons to rejoice in suffering. In Paul's letter to the church in Corinth, he stated that he could "delight" in his struggles because he knew that the Lord's strength was "made perfect in weakness" (2 Corinthians 12:9–10). Paul actually took pleasure in his suffering—even boasted in his suffering—because he had tremendous faith. It was his faith that allowed him to keep an eternal, vertical focus. Paul could rejoice because he wasn't relying on himself but rather on the power of Christ within him as he faced his hardship. It was this reliance and this rejoicing that made Paul an effective soul winner when he was alive and an effective soul winner today through our reading of the Scriptures.

So as you face your storm of infertility, follow the example set by your Savior and His apostle Paul. Rejoice. Rejoice not only *in spite* of your situation but also *because* of your situation. As a result of your faith in this trial, you will be stretched, built up, and strengthened. You will grow in perseverance. So wait upon the Lord. He *is* working. He *is* close at hand. The waiting and the suffering are worth the end result, whatever that result might be.

Again, the childlessness you suffer may appear senseless. Why does God allow our hearts to be broken? Could it be that He allows our hearts to be broken so that He can mend them into something stronger, deeper, fuller? The faith answer is yes. Hold on to the prayer of Habakkuk, which is a beautiful display of his faith.

> Though the fig tree does not bud
>   and there are no grapes on the vines,
> though the olive crop fails
>   and the fields produce no food,
> though there are no sheep in the pen
>   and no cattle in the stalls,
> yet I will rejoice in the LORD,
>   I will be joyful in God my Savior.
> The Sovereign LORD is my strength.
>   (Habakkuk 3:17–19)

Though you may produce no "fruit" in your physical womb, your faith as you move through your difficulty will assuredly produce fruit. Rejoice as this fruit is being produced. Rejoice for the lessons you are being taught. Rejoice for the power that enables you to endure and to live victoriously through your suffering. And, once again, we say, rejoice!

RESURRECTION POWER

Taking refuge in the Rock may be easier said than done, but we want you to contemplate this truth when you experience times of doubt and struggle. The power that raised the solid Rock from death to life is the same power you have access to in your infertility grief. Yes, the resurrection power that rolled the rock away from the tomb is the same power made available to us every day. We can rejoice as we take refuge in the Rock because our suffering offers us the opportunity to tap into this power. God desires the very best for you. He will give you all you need to endure your infertility, and He will reveal Himself to you as you seek refuge in Him. Remember: Your refuge in Him is your freedom. You can be free to quench your thirst by the living water, Jesus, the Christ. *He is your Water from the Rock.*

Application Questions

1. *Have you established a daily quiet time with God? If so, how has this commitment impacted your view of your struggle with infertility?*

2. *When you think of God's love for you, what images come to mind? Are you clinging to His promises of love, or are you deceived by Satan's schemes?*

3. *Who do others say you are? How would you like your trial to refine your character?*

4. *Are you willing to rejoice in your childlessness? Why or why not?*

Victory Verses

But the Lord has become my fortress,
and my God the rock in whom I take refuge.
—PSALM 94:22

They all ate the same spiritual food and drank
the same spiritual drink; for they drank from the spiritual
rock that accompanied them, and that rock was Christ.
—1 CORINTHIANS 10:3–4

Therefore we do not lose heart. Though outwardly we are
wasting away, yet inwardly we are being renewed day by day.
For our light and momentary troubles are achieving
for us an eternal glory that far outweighs them all.
—2 CORINTHIANS 4:16–17

"Every branch that does bear fruit he prunes
so that it will be even more fruitful."
—JOHN 15:2

Now faith is being sure of what we hope for
and certain of what we do not see.
—HEBREWS 11:1

Trust ye in the Lord forever:
for in the Lord Jehovah is everlasting strength.
—ISAIAH 26:4 KJV

FROM HOPE TO ACTION

Taking refuge in the Rock prepares you to produce eternal fruit. Whom can you encourage today in their trial of infertility? Reach out to them with a note, a phone call, or a visit. Send them a copy of *Water from the Rock*. Give them the gift of your growth experience and allow that gift to be a blessing returned to you.

CONCLUSION

A Message from
Donna, Becky, and Phyllis

As you complete the pages of this book, we trust that you have learned about your own grief process and applied these strategies of healing to your life. We three must admit that we have also learned a great deal through the process of writing this book. We have discovered it was just as necessary for us to write this book as for you to read it. We have continued to endure our own individual trials related to infertility. We have made the choice to put into practice what we have been writing about. Our personal results have proved that the strategies in this book will work. We have experienced freedom as we have continued to seek our refuge in the solid rock of Jesus Christ.

We give these words to you to remind you that you are not alone in your struggles. We have felt the emotions you have felt. If we could place an emphasis upon a special thought, it would be that *you would have a calling from God upon your life.*

Scripture tells us that God opens (Genesis 29:31) and closes (1 Samuel 1:6) the womb. His choice is best. Whether He answers your prayers of infertility with or without a child, His power and your purpose are not diminished.

Jeremiah 29:11 says, "For I know the thoughts that I think toward you, saith the Lord, thoughts of peace, and not of evil, to give you an expected end" (KJV). You must believe the promises of God. If He answers your prayers and blesses you with a child or children, then praise be unto His name. God is still a God of miracles, and nothing is impossible for Him. If, on the other hand, it is His will for you to become a spiritual mother of many, then praise still be unto His name. If He gives to you the miracle of ministering to others, He then can birth new life in Christ to other women through you. If you are alive today, it is impossible for you *not* to have a unique, divine life-purpose.

Does this trial you are going through mean that your infertility works to assist God's purpose? Does your infertility work for the good of your brothers and sisters in Christ? Do you allow God to reveal Himself through your infertility? In John 9, we are told about a man born blind. The disciples asked Jesus who had sinned to bring about this punishment of blindness. Jesus answered that no one had sinned. Rather, this man's blindness "happened so that the work of God might be displayed in his life" (v. 3). Likewise, whether our infertility is temporary or permanent, God desires to use it while we have it to glorify Himself. God manifests Himself through the trials in our lives. Will you not allow your storms of life to be used by God as an open book to reveal His glory to others? Whatever your lot in life, be poured out for Him.

God loves you. God has a plan for you. Be still and listen to what He is calling you to do. God picks special people to bear the sorrow of childlessness. On the days when you feel you are going to drown from the height and depth of the seas, remember, God is in control of it all. Daily apply God's Word to your life so that you may become anchored in your storm. Allow the Holy Spirit to clear the muddy waters of your mind and bring you contentment and understanding. As you seek God for the calling in your storm, ask Him for guidance and for a *commission of contentment.*

Why not bow on your knees and pray from your heart the following prayer:

Dear Father God,

I bow before You now, asking Jesus to please take me by the hand and lead me through this journey of infertility into triumph. I do not deny that this trial can stretch my faith and grow my character. Help me to realize that the purpose of my suffering far exceeds the pain of my suffering. Please help me to keep my focus on You, Jesus, and not on my storm. May I realize my calling and the future joys that You have for me. I ask You to guide me in this new life. Show me the change that is required in me, not only to survive my storm of infertility but also to be bold in accepting my calling. Transform my view of infertility. Transform my bondage into freedom. Transform me into a spilled-out vessel of service. May I feel, in a mighty way, Your presence, Your power, and Your peace in my calling and in my life. May the hope of my calling give to me freedom.

In Jesus' name.

Amen

Now, as you begin your journey and the calling of your infertility, look to Jesus for guidance. Keep your eyes on Jesus, and you will survive. Keep your eyes on Jesus, and you will experience victorious joy. Keep your eyes on Jesus, and you will experience abundant living. Keep your eyes on Jesus, and you will experience *water from the rock.*

May our Lord Jesus Christ bless you with the richness of heaven and touch you in such a new way that you will know that you have been in the presence of the Great Physician. Abba, Father.

Your sisters in Christ,

Donna, Becky, and Phyllis

Becky A. Garrett is the Women's Ministry Director for Mud Creek Baptist Church. Her heart is to see women find freedom in Jesus Christ from the hurt of infertility. Becky serves as a facilitator for Vessels of Freedom Ministries. She lives with her husband, Bobby, in Edneyville, North Carolina.

Donna C. Gibbs, a Licensed Professional Counselor and National Certified Counselor, is a member of the American Association of Christian Counselors and practices privately in Hendersonville, North Carolina. She serves on the board of advisors for the Counselor Education program of Western Carolina University, where she received her graduate degree. Donna ministers with Vessels of Freedom and serves together with her husband, Mark, in various marriage enrichment programs.

Phyllis Rabon is an experienced biblical teacher who has spoken extensively for churches and women's and marriage retreats, organized and led numerous Bible studies, and served as a phone counselor for the 700 Club. A former schoolteacher, she is currently vice president of Highly Motivated, Inc., and ministers with Vessels of Freedom. She and her husband, Don, reside in Hendersonville, North Carolina.

The authors of this book are available for speaking engagements. They may be reached through

Vessels of Freedom Ministries
P.O. Box 529
Edneyville, NC 28727
(828) 692-1262, Ext. 117 or Ext. 106
E-mail: BGar443288@cs.com

Press, a ministry of Moody Bible Institute,
or education, evangelization, and edification.
sist you in knowing more about Christ
life, please write us without obligation:
/o MLM, Chicago, Illinois 60610.